01 What Does It Mean To Have A Problem??

I need a lexicographer. Do you know what a lexicographer is?

A lexicographer is a person who writes dictionary definitions.

Write the number 1 on a piece of paper and then write a definition of the word "problem" just like you were writing it for a dictionary.

The following dictionary definition defines a problem more like "not knowing the answer to something. "

> prob·lem n. Abbr. prob. 1. A question to be considered, solved, or answered: math problems; the problem of how to hem a skirt evenly. 2. A situation, matter, or person that presents perplexity or difficulty: urban problems such as traffic congestion and smog; the philosophical problem of evil.

The next useful definition is obstacle. That word is more along the lines of "something that is getting in the way of a person getting something they want." This is probably what many people think of when they use the word problem.

> ob·sta·cle n. One that opposes, stands in the way of, or holds up progress.

Combining the two meanings, we can create a working definition of a problem.

A problem is a situation in which someone or something is keeping a person from getting what they want.

In the movie *Leaving Las Vegas* the characters played by Nicholas Cage and Elizabeth Shue go out for a night of drinking and gambling. Late into the evening, something upsets Cage's character. He tips over a card table and knocks down a waitress. Just as the security people grab him, the scene cuts to Cage sleeping on a sofa.

He awakes with a jolt. His whole body is shaking as he grabs for a bottle of liquor. As he tips it towards his mouth, he discovers that it is empty. The scene then cuts to him kneeling on the floor in front of an open refrigerator. He struggles to open the cap on a fresh bottle of alcohol. His face looks pale and pasty. He is shaking so badly that he can barely pour the alcohol into a carton of orange juice. His face is sweating, and his hands are trembling as he drinks down his mixture.

The scene next cuts to him having the dry heaves in the sink. As the alcohol has its effect, he stops shaking and he shuffles off to bed with Shue's character. He asks her how she managed to keep the security people from throwing him out of the casino into the street. She replies that she told them he was an alcoholic.

Write the number 2 on your paper and then answer this question: Does this man have a problem by your definition? Explain your answer.

If you know the story, you will know that this man had decided to drink himself to death. His problem was that he lived in Los Angeles where the liquor stores closed each night. That was an obstacle for him, because he didn't want to take a chance that he would be without alcohol and go through withdrawal pains. So, he moved to Las Vegas, where the liquor stores are open 24/7. He removed his obstacles. He solved his problem.

Does that change your mind about whether he has a problem or not? Write the number 3 and explain your answer.

Regardless of whether you think he has a problem or not, it does point out that people change because they think they have a problem, not because someone else thinks they do.

And now for something completely different. Write the number 4 on your piece of paper and then write what a person needs to develop if they want to pilot a plane.

Did you write: knowledge, skills, and resources?

> a·bil·i·ty n., pl. a•bil·i·ties. 1. The quality of being able to do something; the physical, mental, financial, or legal power to perform.

You cannot pilot an airplane without the ability to do so.

Write the number 5 on your piece of paper and then answer this question: Can everyone develop the ability to pilot a plane? Explain your answer.

Did you answer - no? They have to have the potential to develop the knowledge, skills, and resources.

For example, they might be blind or not have any arms or legs.

> ca·pac·ity n., pl. ca:pac:i·ties. Abbr. c., C., cap. 5. Innate potential for growth, development, or accomplishment; faculty.

If you lack the capacity to develop the ability, you will be unable to pilot an airplane.

Write the number 6 on your piece of paper and then answer this question: Does everyone with the ability to do something - do it? Explain your answer.

Did you answer no? What else is missing?

They have to want to do it.

> mo·ti·vate tr.v. mo·ti·vat·ed, mo·ti·vat·ing, mo·ti·vates. To provide with an incentive; move to action; impel.

Without motivation, a person will not develop the ability or use it if they have it.

If you want to do something, you have to have the capacity to develop the ability and the desire to develop the ability. Then you have to develop the knowledge, skills, and resources to do it. You just won't get the job done unless you have all of this.

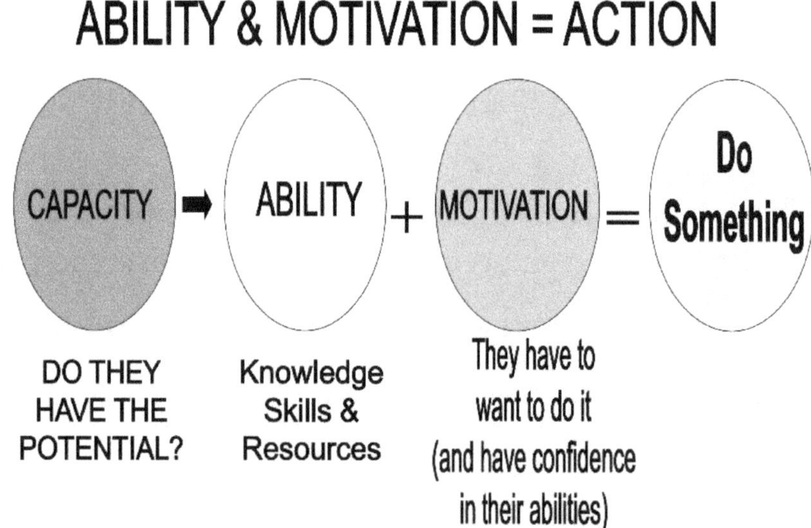

Write the number 7 on your paper and write a paragraph about what the guy in the movie is missing in order to get and stay sober: capacity, motivation, or ability. Why do you think that?

Write the number 8 on your paper and think of one of your problems. Write down what that problem is and then write a paragraph about what area, capacity, motivation, or ability you think you need to work on and why you think that.

02 It Was An Accident - Honest

Write the number 1 on a piece of paper and then write down 5 things that make you angry.

Now, imagine you are driving your car. You go around a corner and hit a big rock in the road and wreck.

Following are some possible explanations:

1) You are driving down the road. You go around the corner and before you have a chance to swerve, you run into a bolder on the road. There was no advance warning that it was there. You didn't intend to hit it.	**A) DELIBERATE**
2) You are driving down the road. There was a notice posted to be on the look out for fallen rocks. You are talking on the cell phone. You go around the corner and you look up to see a bolder on the road, but you do not have a chance to swerve. You run into it, but you could have avoided it had you been paying closer attention. You didn't intend to hit it.	**B) ACCIDENT**
3) You are driving down the road. There was a notice out to be on the look out for fallen rocks. You are speeding. You go around the corner and you see a bolder on the road, but you are going to fast to swerve. You run into it, but you could have avoided it had you been going the speed limit. You didn't intend to hit it.	**C) LACKING KNOWLEDGE AND SKILLS**
4) You are driving down the road. There was a notice out to be on the look out for fallen rocks. You just got your drivers license. You go around the corner and you see a bolder on the road, but you do not know what to do. You run into it. You could have avoided it had you had been a more experienced driver. You didn't intend to hit it.	**D) CARELESS**
5) You are driving down the road. There was a notice posted to be on the look out for fallen rocks. You go around the corner and you see a bolder on the road. You tell yourself "I'll hit it and collect the insurance." You intended to hit it.	**E) RECKLESS**

Now think about what these words mean:

A) DELIBERATE

B) ACCIDENT

C) LACKING KNOWLEDGE AND SKILLS

D) CARELESS

E) RECKLESS

Write the number 2 on your piece of paper. Then write the number of the driving situation and the letter of the word you think matches that situation in the above box. Do that for each situation.

Most people answer this way:

1) (B) ACCIDENT: You are driving down the road. You go around the corner and before you have a chance to swerve, you run into a boulder on the road. There was no advance warning that it was there. You didn't intend to hit it.

2) (D) CARELESS: You are driving down the road. There was a notice out to be on the lookout for fallen rocks. You are talking on the cell phone. You go around the corner, and you look up to see a boulder on the road, but you do not have a chance to swerve. You run into it, but you could have avoided it had you been paying close attention. You didn't intend to hit it.

3) (E) RECKLESS: You are driving down the road. There was a notice out to be on the lookout for fallen rocks. You are speeding. You go around the corner, and you see a boulder on the road, but you are going too fast to swerve. You run into it, but you could have avoided it had you been going the speed limit. You didn't intend to hit it.

4) (C) LACKING KNOWLEDGE AND SKILLS: You are driving down the road. There was a notice out to be on the lookout for fallen rocks. You just got your driver's license. You go around the corner, and you see a boulder on the road, but you do not know what to do. You run into it. You could have avoided it had you had been a more experienced driver. You didn't intend to hit it.

5) (A) DELIBERATE: You are driving down the road. There was a notice out to be on the lookout for fallen rocks. You go around the corner, and you see a boulder on the road. You tell yourself, "I'll hit it and collect the insurance." You intended to hit it.

Here are some common definitions for these words:

An ACCIDENT is something you cannot foresee or avoid.

Being CARELESS means, you are not paying enough attention. (Note that it does not mean that you don't care).

Being RECKLESS means, you are taking an unreasonable chance.

LACKING KNOWLEDGE AND SKILLS means you don't have the ability to do otherwise.

DELIBERATE means you did what you intended to do.

Most people do not get as upset if someone hurts them by accident as they do if someone went out of their way to hurt them on purpose.

Write the number 3 on your piece of paper. Then write the following words on it too:

Careless

Deliberate

Lack of Knowledge or Skills

Reckless

Accident

Then rank the words by their degree of culpability or blameworthiness. Put a 1 next to the act that you feel carries the least blame, a 2 next to the next least blameworthy and so on up to 5 for the act that you feel carries the most blame.

Most people rate it this way:

3 - Careless

5 - Deliberate

2 - Lack of Knowledge or Skills

4 - Reckless

1 -Accident

Now, imagine you were standing in a line minding your own business and someone cuts in front of you.

Write the number 4 on your paper and then write how you think you would feel if someone cut in front of you like that.

Write the number 5 on your paper and then write what you might think about the person who cut in front of you.

Write the number 6 on your paper and write what you might do in response to someone cutting in line.

These are some of the things they might have been thinking when they cut in line:

1) The person who cut in line was thinking, "I had better hurry and get in line." They are in such a hurry that they do not even notice that they cut in front of you. If they had, they wouldn't have done it.

A) DELIBERATE

2) The person who cut in line was thinking, "I'll cut in front of that guy. He's such a wimp, he'll be too afraid to say anything."

B) ACCIDENT

3) The person who cut in line was thinking, "I'll cut in front of that guy. He'll probably won't mind. If he says anything, I'll move back." The guy does mind and a fight results.

C) LACKING KNOWLEDGE AND SKILLS

4) The guy who cut in line was thinking, "The teacher said that I get to be at the front of the line." However, the teacher forgot that she told someone else that they could be up front. The teacher may have been careless, but the guy who acted on her information thought everything was ok.

D) CARELESS

5) The guy who cut in line was thinking, I'll just go to the front of the line." No one had taught him that cutting in line was bad manners.

E) RECKLESS

Think about these words again:

A) DELIBERATE

B) ACCIDENT

C) LACKING KNOWLEDGE AND SKILLS

D) CARELESS

E) RECKLESS

Write the number 7 on your piece of paper. Then write the number of the cut-in-line situation and the letter of the label you think matches that situation. Do this for each situation.

Most people answer this way:

1) (D) CARELESS: The person who cut in line was thinking, "I had better hurry and get in line." They are in such a hurry that they do not even notice that they cut in front of you. If they had, they wouldn't have done it.

2) (A) DELIBERATE: The person who cut in line was thinking, "I'll cut in front of that guy. He's such a wimp, he'll be too afraid to say anything."

3) (E) RECKLESS: The person who cut in line was thinking, "I'll cut in front of that guy. He will probably not mind. If he says anything, I'll move back." The guy does mind, and a fight results.

4) (B) ACCIDENT: The guy who cut in line was thinking, "The teacher said that I get to be at the front of the line." However, the teacher forgot that she told someone else that they could be up front. The teacher may have been careless, but the guy who acted on her information thought everything was ok and had no way of knowing different.

5) (C) LACKING KNOWLEDGE AND SKILLS: The guy who cut in line was thinking, "I'll just go to the front of the line." No one had taught him that cutting in line was bad manners.

Remember that:

An ACCIDENT is something you cannot foresee or avoid.

Being CARELESS means, you are not paying enough attention. (Remember, it doesn't mean you don't care.)

Being RECKLESS means, you are taking an unreasonable chance.

LACKING KNOWLEDGE AND SKILLS means you don't have the ability to do otherwise.

DELIBERATE means you did what you intended to do.

Write the number 8 on your paper and then write about what you see as the disadvantages of acting before you know what is really going on when you are angry about something (like someone cutting in line in front of you).

Write the number 9 on your piece of paper and then write the letter of the reason listed below for the way you acted the last time you got really angry at someone, and did something you regretted later:

A) ACCIDENT (outcome was unforeseeable and unavoidable)

B) CARELESS (not paying enough attention. It does not mean you don't care)

C) RECKLESS (took an unreasonable risk)

D) LACKING KNOWLEDGE AND SKILLS (did not know how to deal with it effectively)

E) DELIBERATE (did what you intended to do)

Write the number 10 on your piece of paper and then write a sentence or two about why you think you responded that way. What were your thoughts about the person?

Write the number 11 on your piece of paper and then write a sentence or two about why losing your temper is not an accident, if you know the kind of stuff that makes you angry or if you act before you know what is really going on.

Write the number 12 on your piece of paper and write whether you think avoiding problems is a matter of willpower (motivation) or whether a person also needs knowledge and skills. Explain your answer.

Here are some knowledge and skill development tools:

1. Understanding the differences between people.

2. Knowing my triggers (things that I get angry about).

3. Knowing ways to manage my emotions.

4. Knowing when I am getting worked up before I do anything I'll regret later.

5. Knowing how to calm down.

6. Knowing how to deal with stress.

7. Changing beliefs that seem right, but that get me into trouble.

8. Having a clear idea about what is important to me.

9. Keeping in mind those things that are important to me so that I don't do anything to harm them.

10. How to solve problems without making more problems later.

11. How to let go of things that I want but cannot have.

12. How to communicate well enough so that other people really understand me.

13. How to stop blaming other people for things I do.

14. How to set goals.

15. How to stick to my plans and not get sidetracked.

16. How to keep from doing stupid things because of alcohol or other drugs.

17. How to relax.

Write the number 13 on your piece of paper. Then pick 3 of those knowledge and skill development tools that you think would help you the most with keeping out of trouble in the future. Write their numbers down and then explain why you think they would help.

03 Bicameral Mind

A very funny movie is *All of Me* starring Steve Martin and Lily Tomlin. In the movie, Tomlin's character plays a rich woman who has been sickly all of her life. She is about to die and has hired a swami, a holy man from India, to take her soul from her body, put it in a brass container, take the soul out of a young healthy woman and release it to the cosmos and then put Tomlin's soul into the young healthy body so she gets another shot at life.

Of course, something goes very wrong. Tomlin's consciousness and Martin's consciousness both end up inside Martin's body. The sight gags that follow are hilarious as Tomlin tries to get Martin's body to do one thing and Martin tries to do something else.

Of course, it is impossible to have two people inside of one body. However, it sometimes seems that we have two people inside of us. One that feels we should do one thing and another that thinks we should do something else. Often this leads us to do things that we regret later. Why is that?

To answer this question, we first need to understand a little about how the human mind makes decisions.

We have two minds. One is automatic and driven by emotional urges. And another that is deliberate and rational. Our two minds sometimes struggle with each other trying to win us over.

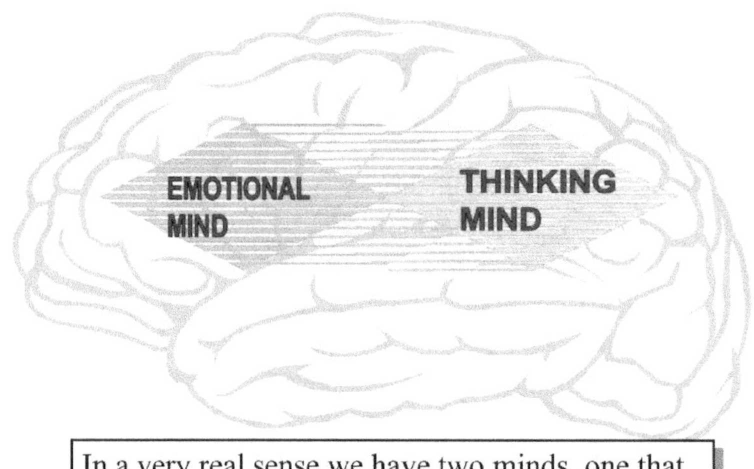

In a very real sense we have two minds, one that thinks and one that feels.

Emotional Intelligence
Daniel Goleman

Perhaps you experienced a struggle of this nature the last time you were thinking about buying a new car. Part of you wanted the little red sports car. Sports cars are fast, sexy, and really really neat. You just had to have it. However, another part of you wanted to slow down and think things through before you decided what to buy. "How much would it cost? What kind of gas mileage would it get? How much would insurance be? Would it be hard to get repairs?"

For the most part, our two minds work together harmoniously to decide how we should respond to life's events, but not always. Many personal problems can be understood as a conflict between the two minds and a person's inability to resolve this conflict in favor of the best deal under the circumstances.

The emotional mind processes information and makes decisions automatically and is experienced through emotional feelings.

The emotional mind is:

Impatient (urges you to act right away)

Closed-Minded (makes you stubbornly unreceptive to ideas that differ from how you feel)

Short-Sighted (makes you concerned with only the immediate future)

Single-Minded (makes you concerned with only the immediate concern)

If your emotional mind has determined that something undesirable is about to happen, your brain normally prepares you to fight the threat or run away from it. This is called the "fight or flight response". If your emotional mind decides to put a stop to the menace, it prepares to confront it with intimidation or force, and you experience anger or a related emotion.

If, on the other hand, your emotional mind concludes that it probably cannot stop the threat, it prepares your body for escape, and you experience fear or a related emotion.

The emotional mind is built up from gut feelings, past experiences, and beliefs.

1. **Gut Feelings**: With gut feelings, people are predisposed to respond to some things in a certain way, because that is how their brains are wired. You don't have to be taught to be afraid of tigers or feel-good inside when a baby smiles at you. That's just part of being human.

2. **Past Experiences**: The emotional mind is also driven by experience. Once a person has had an emotionally significant experience, they tend to feel the same way later in similar situations and are emotionally urged to respond as they did then. We learn through experience what things cause pain and pleasure and use those experiences as guides for future behavior.

3. **Beliefs**: The emotional mind also operates with habitual beliefs. People form generalized ideas that explain how the world works, how they personally should act in certain situations and how other people should behave in certain situations. If those thoughts are repeated frequently, they become automatic

beliefs, and a person feels urged to act as they direct without having to consciously think them first.

The way the emotional mind makes decisions and solves problems is by telling you that:

This is what is going on.

This is what you should do about it.

It is automatic processing. There is no thinking. There are no choices, things just flow. The emotional mind offers a solution for the situation at hand, the surface problem, without consideration for anything else that might be important to you.

The thinking mind, on the other hand, is slower than the emotional mind. Often the emotional mind has already urged a response before the thinking mind has even begun to register the situation. Furthermore, the thinking mind is often less certain and intense than the emotional mind.

The thinking mind uses deliberate (nonautomatic) information processing and decision making and is experienced through conscious verbal thoughts and images.

The thinking mind is:

Patient (it does not urge you to act right away).

Open-minded (it makes you receptive to new ideas).

Long-ranged (it makes you concerned about the immediate future and the long-term future).

Global-minded (it makes you concerned about all the things that are important to you).

Your thinking mind makes decisions by problem-solving or coping. It decides by asking:

What is really going on?

What are my options?

What is the best deal under the circumstances?

This is a list of Feeling or Thinking characteristics:

1) Long ranged (concerned with immediate future and long term)

2) Fast

3) Impatient (urged to act right away)

4) Unquestioned sense of certainty

5) Tentative

6) Intense/Excited

7) Patient (not urged to act right away)

8) Open-minded (receptive to new ideas)

9) Single-Minded (only concerned with immediate wants)

10) Slow

11) Closed-Minded (stubbornly unreceptive to new ideas)

12) Short-Sighted (only concerned with immediate future)

13) Global-minded (concerned with all of your wants and needs)

14) Calm

Write the numbers 1 through 14 on a piece of paper. Then look at the Feeling or Thinking characteristics list. If you think a characteristic is one that belongs to the emotional mind, put the letter E next to the number. If you think it belongs to the thinking mind, put a T next to the number.

Did you answer this way?

1) T. Thinking Mind: Long ranged (concerned with immediate future and long term)

2) E. Emotional Mind: Fast

3) E. Emotional Mind: Impatient (urged to act right away)

4) E. Emotional Mind: Unquestioned sense of certainty

5) T. Thinking Mind: Tentative

6) E. Emotional Mind: Intense/Excited

7) T. Thinking Mind: Patient (not urged to act right away)

8) T. Thinking Mind: Open-minded (receptive to new ideas)

9) E. Emotional Mind: Single-Minded (only concerned with immediate wants)

10) T. Thinking Mind: Slow

11) E. Emotional Mind: Closed-Minded (stubbornly unreceptive to new ideas)

12) E. Emotional Mind: Short-Sighted (only concerned with immediate future)

13) T. Thinking Mind: Global-minded (concerned with all of your wants and needs)

14) T. Thinking Mind: Calm

Even though the emotional mind is faster, more intense and has a greater unquestioned sense of certainty than the thinking mind, the thinking mind has the potential, in most cases, to direct a person's behavior. This is basically for 2 reasons:

1. Emotional urges only last for a few seconds. If the stimulus disappears, the emotion fades quickly.

2. It is a person's thoughts that can keep an emotion active long after the original stimulus is gone.

Emotions Only Last a Few Seconds (unless retriggered)

Man is not disturbed by events, but by the view he takes of them.

Epictetus

To give an example of this, imagine that you are in heavy traffic. A car cuts in front of you and then heads off an exit ramp. You might have an initial gut reaction of fear, but it fades in seconds.

However, you might start thinking: "That blankety blank SOB. Who does he think he is? I'd like to teach that little @#&* a thing or two." If you think like that, you will create angry feelings and emotional urges to punish the perpetrator. If you keep those thoughts up, you will put yourself into a bad mood, striking out at other people without good cause.

On the other hand, you might stop your initial angry thoughts and replace them with self-controlling thoughts. "I'm not gonna let that spoil my day." If you do this, you will calm down and your mood and thoughts will return to normal.

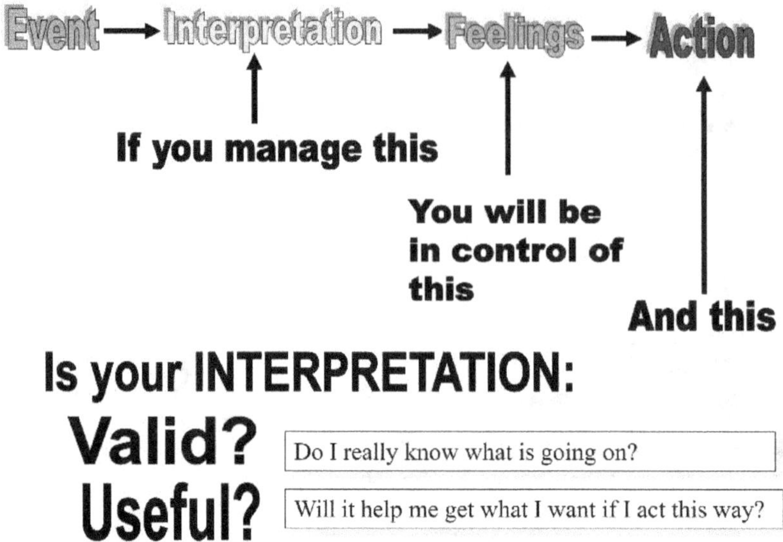

It was the same event, a car cutting in front of you. What made a difference in how you felt was not the event, but how you explained it to yourself.

Ask yourself:

Is my interpretation valid and useful?

Do I really know what is going on?

Will it help me get what I want if I act this way?

Your thinking mind has the capacity to be in charge of your emotional mind. However, there are ways in which the emotional mind gets the upper hand. These are called dysreasoning effects.

Here are some dysreasoning effects":

1. **Impulsivity Temperament**: Some people are prone to impulsiveness; their emotional mind jumps them into action before their thinking mind even has a chance to get started. People of this temperament are not only impulsive but trust their impulses and feel frustrated if they are restrained from acting on them, even if doing so has been a source of problems for them in the past.

In addition, people under stress tend to be impulsive, regardless of their temperament. When you are stressed, you cannot think clearly and are driven by how you feel and not by reason.

2. **Emotional Hijacking**: Another dysreasoning effect is an emotional hijacking. Some situations get people so emotionally overwhelmed that they cannot think straight, and they let their emotions carry them away. When their emotional mind declares an emergency, their thinking mind's ability to function is compromised. Acting in a rage is an example. After a person calms down and reason returns, they wonder what came over them.

3. **Clouded Judgment**: Clouded judgment is another dysreasoning effect. Rather than seeking evidence for their interpretation of events, they just feel blindly confident that they know what is going on. Rather than formulating a variety of choices, they only create options consistent with their current state of emotions. Their moods bias their decision-making. When a person is sad, for example, they lose confidence in their abilities and do not attempt activities they might normally pursue.

4. **Irrational Beliefs**: Beliefs of this type limit a person's thinking by providing irrational, inflexible responses to life's situations, instead of developing effective solutions. Rather than being resilient and creative, they do things a certain way every time, whether that way is useful or not. "This is too awful; I can't stand it."

5. **Avoidance Strategies**: The emotions we often experience when things are not going our way are anger, sadness, fear, and anxiety. These emotions can bias a person's thoughts and lead to the development of habitual avoidance strategies that result in their neglecting the sources of their problems.

A person's thoughts might be: "This is awful and there is nothing I can do about it." Those thoughts might make a person feel **SAD** and see themselves as powerless. As a result, they will just give up and do nothing to solve their problems.

A person might think: "This is bad, and I don't know what to do." This will make them feel **ANXIOUS** and ruminate, rather than act.

A person might think: "This is awful. I've just got to get away." These thoughts will make them experience **FEAR** and feel like running away, literally or in their heads. They can easily rationalize, minimize, intellectualize, and procrastinate rather than trying to solve their problems.

They might have thoughts like: "This is not fair. The'll pay for doing that." Some people feel **ANGRY** and see others as the source of their problems. They will believe that others need to change, not themselves, before a situation can get better. As a result, they will not take constructive actions to solve their problems.

Some **ANGRY** people become aggressive and risk retribution from others.

6. **Palliative Relief**: People sometimes do things that make them feel good, at least temporarily, but that do not address the source of the problem. They overeat, gamble, shop, or use alcohol and other drugs. They may do something that makes them feel dominant and powerful. They kick the dog or yell at the kids.

7. **Alcohol & Other Drugs**: Alcohol and other drugs can also lead to a dysreasoning effect by altering brain functions. While alcohol and other drugs affect all brain functioning, they tend to diminish higher cognitive functions, turning off the thinking mind, quicker and to a greater extent than they do the emotional mind.

8. **Mental Disorder**: Mental disorders may also be a dysreasoning effect, because they can distort a person's ideas about reality.

To be in control of your life, you need to eliminate any dysreasoning effects that get in the way of clear thinking.

This is a list of clear-thinking tools:

Value Clarification

Refuting Irrational Beliefs

Management of Emotions

Problem-Solving

Relaxation Training

Recognizing Problem Areas and Response Rehearsals

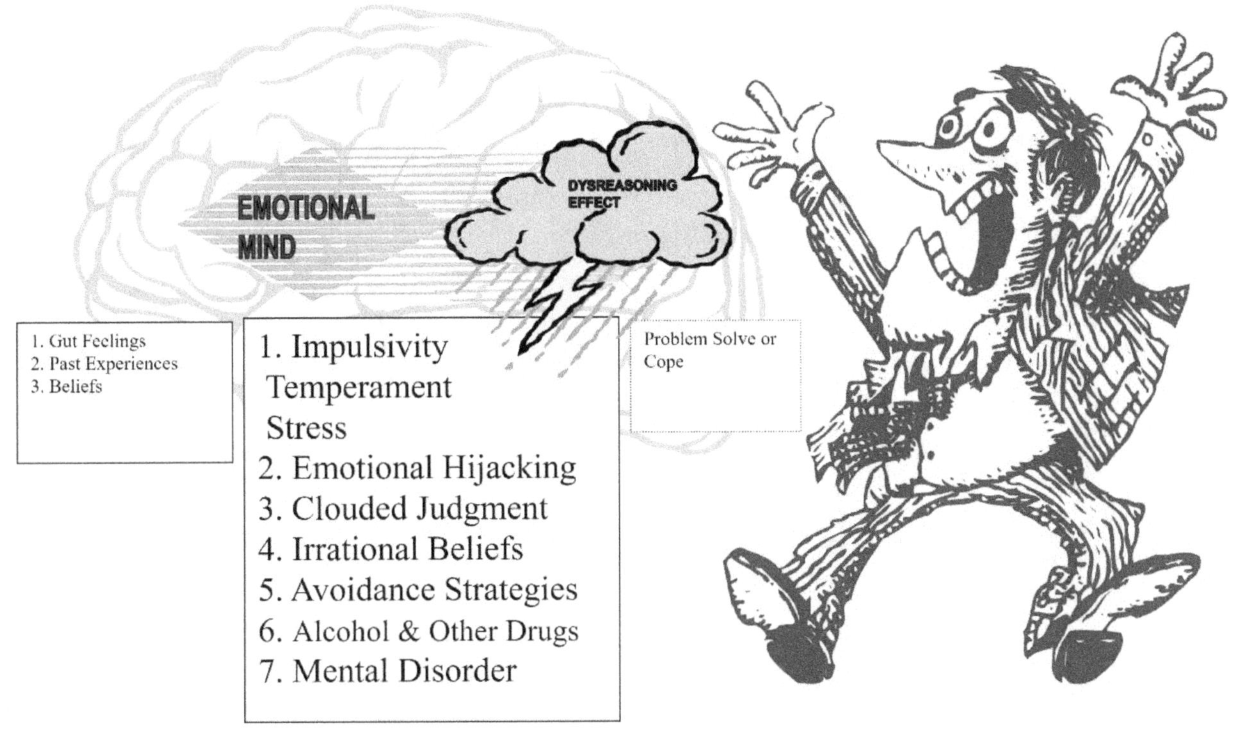

Write the number 15 on your piece of paper. Then write a sentence or two on what you think each of these techniques are and how they might help eliminate dysreasoning effects.

Write the number 16 on your piece of paper. Then write a sentence or two on which of these techniques you think would be most useful for you to use more often and why.

04 What Is Important To You?

Write the numbers 1 through 10 on a piece of paper. Now write 10 things in your life that you love to do or would love to do someday or things that you love possessing or would love to have some day. They can be big things or little things. They can be concrete things (things that you can see and touch, like a car) or abstract things (things you can only think and feel about like justice).

Now put a dollar sign ($) next to the left of each item on your list that costs money to do or have.

Put the letter "A" on the left side beside each item that you prefer to do alone or not to share.

Put the letter "O" beside each item that you prefer to do with others or to share.

Put the letter "P" next to those things that require planning to do or to obtain.

Place an "L" next to those things that you think will likely still be on your list a long time from now.

List 10 Things that You Value

$ 1.
  2.
A 3.
  4.
O 5.
  6.
P 7.
  8.
L 9.
  10.

Now circle the top 3 things you value the most.

Getting what you want does not necessarily mean you are self-centered. We may want things for others. Look at your list of values. Are any of them things you want for others? If not add one.

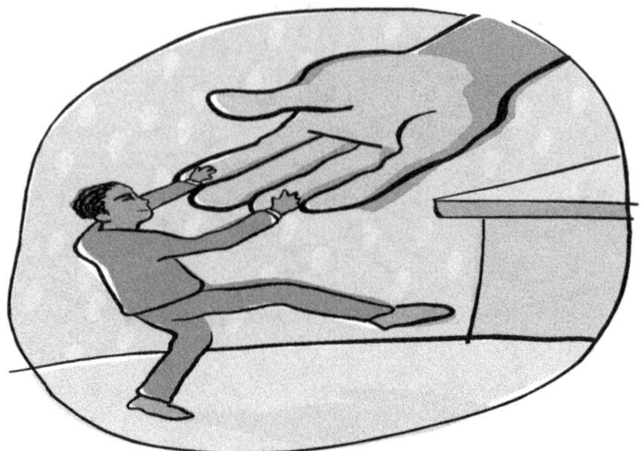

We value things (objects and experiences) that we believe will help us feel good or things that we believe will help free us from things we don't like.

The things we have and want and how we go about getting and keeping them can cause us problems.

WANTS

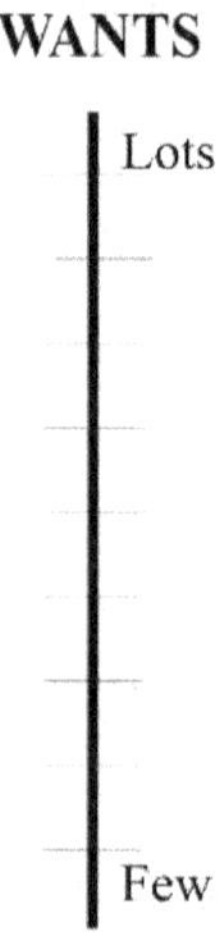

This chart represents all of the things we value. If we have a lot of things that we want to keep in our lives and if we want a lot of things that we don't yet have, we are at the top of the line. If we don't value many things, we would be at the bottom of the line.

People will have difficulties in life if the things they want are unrealistic and incompatible.

Unrealistic wants are things we want that we cannot realistically obtain. No matter how competent you are, if you want something you cannot realistically obtain, you will fail and then feel bad. An example of a want that is not realistic might be wanting to do whatever you want to do regardless of the law and expecting to be left alone.

Write the number 11 on your paper and list 3 other examples of unrealistic wants.

Incompatible haves and wants, on the other hand, cause you to want things that clash. When you get one, you screw up the others. An example of a want that is not compatible with other things a person values might be liking Meth, but also liking freedom. If they use, they risk losing their freedom.

Write the number 12 on your paper and list 3 other examples of incompatible haves and wants.

Look at your values list again. Are any of them unrealistic? Are there things on your list that are incompatible with other more important things? Write the number 13 on your paper and then write your answer to these questions and explain why you think that way.

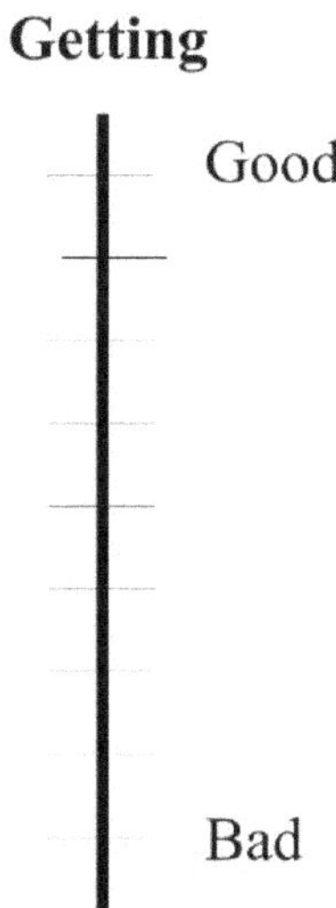

This chart represents our ability to get and keep those things we have and want. If we are doing a good job getting what we want, we are at the top of the line. If we are doing a poor job, we are at the bottom of the line.

If we put the two charts together, we can have a graphic representation of what goes on in our lives when we are getting the things we want and when we are not.

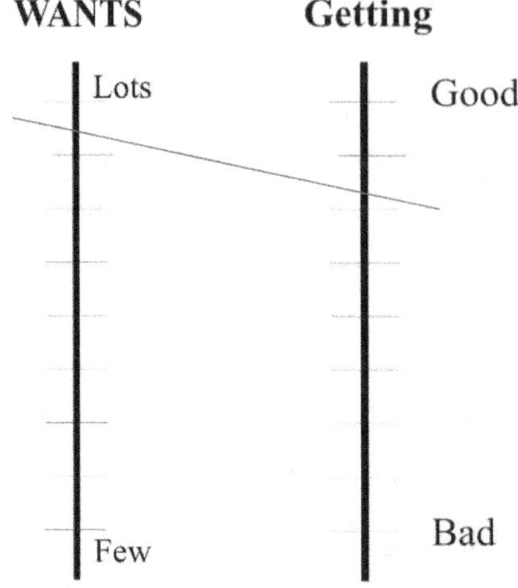

Write the number 14 on your paper. Then write how you feel when your overall haves and wants match you getting and keeping? Or, in other words, when you are doing a good job at getting what you want.

Did you write things like these?

Power

Control

Elation

Pleasure

Satisfaction

Joy

Write the number 15 on your paper. Then write how you feel when you are not doing a good job at getting what you want.

Did you write things like these?

Sad

Angry

Afraid

Worried

Unfulfilled

Discontented

Sometimes we have problems in life because of the way we go about getting what we want. For example, a person may want friends but tries too hard and drive people away.

Sometimes people don't get what they want because they let their emotions get in the way. For example, a person may want a good job but gets mad at the interviewer and calls him an idiot when he questions you about something on your application. Write the number 16 on your paper and then list 3 other examples of not getting what you want because of emotions.

Look at your values list again. Are there things on it that you are not getting because of the way you go about trying to get them? If so, which things? Is that because you are:

Careless (not paying enough attention)

Reckless (taking too many chances)

Don't know how to get what you want without creating other problems

Too impulsive

Alcohol or other drugs use is interfering with clear thinking

Poor problem-solving skills

Write the number 17 on your paper and then your answers to these questions, along with why you think this is so.

No one gets what they want all the time. Sometimes you do things that don't turn out the way you wanted. Sometimes other people interfere. Sometimes what you want messes up something else you want.

When you are not getting what you want, you have three choices:

Problem-Solve

Cope

Muddle-Through

Problem-solving means fixing the problem so that you get what you want, either now or the next time. You change those things outside of you. An example of problem-solving might be that you are late for work a lot because you oversleep, so you buy an alarm clock.

Remember when we talked about dysreasoning effects? Dysreasoning effects interfere with good problem-solving. If you are having problems, dysreasoning effects must be dealt with.

Dysreasoning Effects:

Impulsivity (temperament/stress)

Emotional Hijacking

Clouded Judgment

Irrational Beliefs

Avoidance Strategies

Alcohol and Other Drugs

Mental Disorder

There are times when you are not getting what you want, and you cannot fix it. Coping is changing how we feel inside, so that we can live with something we cannot change. It means cutting yourself loose from something you cannot have, so that not having it does not haunt you. You just don't want it anymore.

Coping means getting rid of unrealistic wants and reprioritizing your haves and wants.

These ideas are nothing new. They are exemplified in the Serenity Prayer.

God grant me the serenity to accept the things I cannot change (which means coping). Courage to change the things I can (which means problem-solving). And the wisdom to know the difference.

Muddling-through is the last option. Muddling-through means that a person is not getting what they want, they don't like what is going on, but they do not do anything to change and make their lives better. They just wait out the bad experience and hope things will get better.

For example, you have a coworker who is very bossy, but is not the boss. Rather than complain to the real boss, or accept the coworker for what he is, you just gripe all the time.

People often muddle-through rather than problem solve or cope. For example, a person may go drinking when they have a fight with their partner. Write the number 18 on your paper and then list 3 examples of muddling-through.

Write the number 19 on your paper and then write why you think people sometimes muddle-through rather than problem solve or cope?

There is also a type of muddling-through called the Phantom-Fix. It involves not getting what you want, not liking that you are not getting it, but not taking steps to problem-solve or to cope. Rather you do something that makes you feel good, so that you forget about the problem for a while, but whatever it is that you are doing to make yourself feel good is only making the real problem worse.

Write the number 20 on your paper and then list 3 examples of people using a phantom fix.

Did you write things like:

Drinking

Using drugs

Gambling

Shopping

Overeating

Doing something that makes you feel powerful

If a person makes a habit of not dealing with problems very well, one of three things can happen. One is that they can go for years muddling-through, not getting what they want, and feeling bad. Or they can take the phantom-fix and feel good for a little while and then bad and then good and then bad. And so on. Then in the meantime, their problems keep getting worse and worse. Their problems become more intense. They become more frequent. They last longer. They start to spread into other areas of their lives and the temporary good feelings get smaller and smaller.

Or they can start giving up the things they value. For example, "If my wife doesn't want me to drink. I'll get rid of her." Or "If my boss keeps giving me a hard time about being late, I'll just quit." Eventually, they have given up most of the things that they value. Then they don't feel bad, they feel numb.

Do you know someone like this?

Do you remember when we recently discussed avoidance strategies? This is when people muddle-through because their emotions are telling them to ignore their problems. If you have problems and are muddling-through, you need to eliminate any avoidance strategies or phantom fixes you might be using. You need to start problem-solving or coping, otherwise, all of your problems will get worse and worse.

Here are some situations and labels that might go with those situations:

1) "I really wanted that job. That interviewer was a jerk. They all are. What's the point of trying?"

2) "I really wanted that job. I'll finish my GED. That'll help the next time there is an opening."

3) "I really wanted that job. Screw it. I'm getting high."

4) "I really wanted that job, but someone else got it. That's life I guess."

5) "I really wanted that job. How am I going to pay my bills? I don't want to think about it."

6) "I really wanted that job. Damn it." Then he kicks the dog.

A) **Muddling-through** by ignoring the problem.

B) **Coping** (Changing how you feel on the inside in a useful way)

C) **Problem Solving** (fixing the problem)

D) **Phantom Fix** (doing something that makes you feel powerful so that you don't think about your problems)

E) **Muddling-through** using blame (not seeing self as part of the problem)

F) **Phantom Fix** (doing something that makes you temporary feel good, but doesn't fix the problem)

Write the number 21 on your piece of paper. Then write the number of the situation and the letter of the label you think matches that situation.

Did you answer this way:

> 1) (E) Muddling-through using blame (not seeing self as part of the problem) "I really wanted that job. That interviewer was a jerk. They all are. What's the point of trying?"
>
> 2) (C) Problem-Solving (fixing the problem) "I really wanted that job. I'll finish my GED. That'll help the next time there is an opening."

3) (D) Phantom Fix (doing something that makes you temporarily feel good but doesn't fix the problem) "I really wanted that job. Screw it. I'm getting high."

4) (B) Coping (changing how you feel on the inside in a useful way) "I really wanted that job, but someone else got it. That's life, I guess. There's always next time."

5) (A) Muddling-through by ignoring the problem. "I really wanted that job. How am I going to pay my bills? I don't want to think about it."

6) (D) Phantom Fix (doing something that makes you feel powerful so that you don't think about your problems) "I really wanted that job. Dammit." Then he kicks the dog.

We must face our bad feelings and problem-solve or cope. In doing so, the problem will be gone, and we will feel better in a way that maintains the stability and integrity of all of the things we value.

Write the number 22 on your paper and then write one of the things you value that you are not currently getting? Then write how that makes you feel. Write what you think about not getting it? Then write how you are dealing with it:

Problem-Solving

Coping

Muddling-through (blaming)

Avoidance Strategies

Phantom Fix

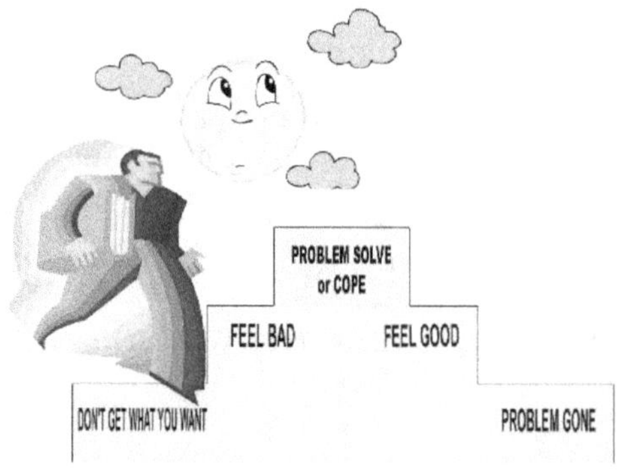

05 The Management Of Emotions

Imagine that you are sitting in a jeep on a muddy road. You are surrounded by a lush green jungle. There are plants and trees of all kinds. It is hot and steamy. Your friend is in the jungle and while you are waiting, the only sounds you hear come from the birds as they busily call each other.

You feel a faint tremor and wonder if it is an earthquake, though it felt too mild. Another tremor shortly follows. The call of the birds is replaced by the rush of wings as they take flight and darken the sky. The tremors continue. They are too regular to be aftershocks. You hear a distant rustling sound and then a snap. The tremors feel stronger. You feel the snaps now as well as hear them. The noises grow louder. The cracking sounds vaguely remind you of something breaking. "My god", you think, "something is snapping the trees and it's coming this way."

Just then you hear your friend's voice screaming out in terror. "Get out of here. Get out of here." Over and over again, "Get out of here."

Your heart begins to pound out of your chest. "My god, what's going on? What should I do?"

"Get out of here. It's coming after me. Get out of here."

You start the jeep just as your friend jumps out onto the road behind you. Suddenly you hear a terrible screeching sound. It is so frightening that you freeze. "My god what was that?"

Your friend screams, "Help me, please help me."

You put the jeep in reverse, and it jumps backward and dies. As you fumble with the keys, your friend leaps into the back of the jeep. "Get out of here. It's right behind me."

You look in the mirror only to see it filled with the huge head of some terrible beast sticking out from the tops of the trees. It is gray and savage looking. It turns its head sideways and aims a single eye at you. Another screech. Its mouth is full of dagger-like teeth. You restart the jeep and speed off. It screeches again and comes after you. Your emotions are going wild.

Once you got away, you calmed down.

> # An emotion is a feeling inside of us that urges us to act in a way that nature has selected to be in our (immediate) best interest.

An emotion is a feeling inside of us that urges us to act in a way that nature has selected to be in our immediate best interest.

Write the number 1 on a piece of paper and then write down 25 emotions.

One idea that helps explain why people do what they do is that they tend to act in ways that they feel will get them what they want and that avoid what they don't want. They seek out and do things that they have found will make them feel good or seek out and do things that will free them from things that they have found will make them feel bad.

On your piece of paper, write a plus sign (+) behind each of the emotions you listed that makes you feel good and a minus sign (-) behind each emotion that makes you feel bad.

When something happens or is about to happen that we believe is going to hurt us in some way, our bodies instinctively respond with what is called the "fight or flight" response.

The fight or flight response is a way nature helps us deal with threats. We either force the source of the threat to stop or we run away from it.

Fight or Flight

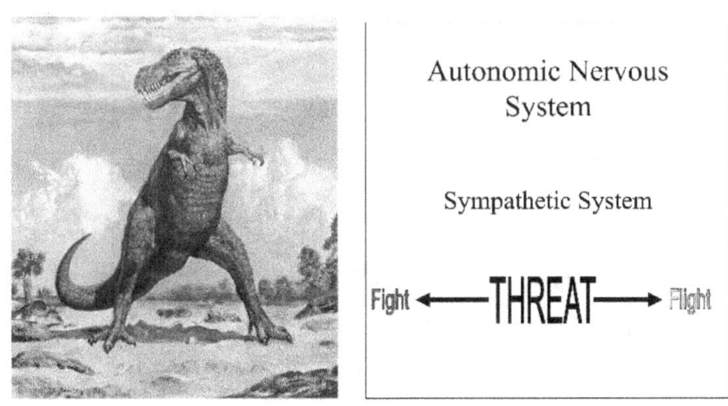

The fight or flight response gears the body up to deal with threats.

One of the first things that happens when you feel threatened is that your heart starts to beat faster. Your muscles need fuel and oxygen to work and that is supplied by your blood. If you are going to run or fight, your muscles are going to have to work at their best, so your heart automatically beats faster to pump more blood to your muscles. It is all part of the fight or flight response.

If you are going to fight or run away, your muscles are going to need oxygen. Oxygen helps your muscles get more miles to the gallon, so to speak. So, your lungs begin to work faster so you have more endurance and don't poop out during a life and death struggle.

Another thing that happens is that you begin to sweat. If you are going to fight or if you are going to run, your muscles will produce heat and hot muscles don't work well. Sweat helps get rid of the extra heat. If you have ever been nervous, the palms of your hands get sweaty and sweat breaks out on your forehead. It all happens automatically as part of the fight or flight response.

Blood is directed to the muscles and away from parts of the body that are not crucial to running or fighting. You can digest your lunch later, but now you have to fight. The blood vessels to the muscles open bigger while they narrow to unnecessary organs, like the digestive system. The blood is directed to where it will be needed. This is why we feel butterflies in our stomachs and our mouth becomes dry when we become excited.

Adrenaline is nature's own methamphetamines. When it is released into the blood it stimulates the brain and senses so that we can respond more keenly to situations as they develop. Adrenalin also tells the liver to release sugar into the blood stream for extra fuel. It also tells fat cells to release fat for even more fuel. This is why we feel excited when something threatening is going on. It's getting us ready to fight or take flight.

Endorphins are released into the body. Endorphins are nature's own morphine like pain killers. If you are going to run or fight, you are going to experience pain. Endorphins are released to kill the pain before it even occurs. It's nature's way of keeping us from giving up.

Finally, our muscles tense. This is believed to happen for a few reasons. One is that it braces you for an attack. Another is that when your muscles are tense, you stand up straighter and as a result look bigger and more threatening to whatever is threatening you. And tight muscles make your muscles become armor to protect important stuff inside your body.

Fight or Flight

We have already discussed fleeing or fighting as two main strategies associated with threatening situations. There are two other strategies for dealing with threatening situations.

If we want to do something about a threat, but cannot decide what to do, we run it around in our head, ruminating on the problem. It's nature's way of keeping us on task until we decide to do something.

Also, if we think that nothing can eliminate the threat, we surrender and do nothing. Sometimes struggling makes things worse, so it is better to not fight back and to go off and lick our wounds. Our body language signals to our family and friends that we need help, and they often come to our aid.

While there aren't any dinosaurs anymore, anytime someone is rude, insults you, treats you unjustly, is demeaning or frustrates you (intentionally or unintentionally) all of the fight or flight responses are triggered. This is the cause of much of the stress we experience in everyday life.

There are emotions associated with these behaviors.

If we feel **fear**, we act to get away from the threat by fleeing, either literally or in our heads.

If we feel **angry**, we act to eliminate the threat by intimidation or force.

When we don't know what to do about a threat, we feel **worried** and freeze. Worry urges us to figure out what to do. It bugs us to stay on task.

If we think that nothing can eliminate the threat, we feel **sadness** and do nothing. Sadness urges us to pull back, to reflect on our problems; and it can sometimes get others to help us.

Now get another piece of paper and make a chart like this on it. Then go through your list of emotions, pick out all the feel bad emotions and write them on your chart next to emotions to which they are most closely related. For example, rage would probably go next to anger and grief would probably go next to sadness.

If nature has selected our emotions as the way we should respond to problems, then shouldn't we just go with the flow?

Consider the following exchange between a husband and his wife:

"Where have you been? You were supposed to be home an hour ago."

"They had a sale on kids' clothes, and I was just looking for some stuff for the baby."

"Who did you talk to?"

"No one. I was just shopping. That's all."

"I know how you are. Give me your car keys."

"No, Ron, I need them. Please."

"Don't talk back to me, you bitch."

"Oh god, please Ron. You promised. Please don't. ... "

"Whore. Who do you think you're fooling?"

"Please don't hit me, Ron. I was just shopping."

"You dirty slut. Ain't I good enough for you?"

"Oh, please Ron. It was .... Oh god, stop. Please stop."

"I'll teach you; you bitch."

"Stop it. Please stop it. ..."

When she woke up the next morning there were a dozen roses beside her on the bed.

Write the number 2 on another piece of paper and then answer these questions:

Why did he bring her the flowers?

What emotion do you think he was experiencing when he was hitting her?

If he was angry, what might he have thought was a threat to him?

What advantage might hitting her offer him?

What disadvantage might that behavior cause him?

Do you think his behavior got him what he wanted in the short run? Explain your answer.

Do you think his behavior will get him what he wants in the long run? Explain your answer.

If you run away from a dinosaur, you solved your problem. If you run away from a problem with your spouse, either literally by leaving the house or figuratively by not dealing with it, your problems are still there waiting for you.

If you killed the dinosaur, you solved your problem. If you hit your spouse, you've got more problems.

Think about a time when you experienced emotions so strong that you did something that you regretted later. Who were you with? What time was it? Was it day or night? Were you inside or out? Were you warm or cold? Were there any sounds in the background? Write the number 3 on your paper and then write a paragraph about that incident.

Emotions can cause us to do things we may regret later. It would be better if we maintained some control over them. However, some people think that how you feel is how you feel and that emotions cannot be changed. Let me tell you a little story and we will see if we can answer that.

Imagine that it is a really cold winter's night - well below zero. There was a huge snowstorm earlier in the day and much of the city is not yet dug out. You have already gotten into bed and are nice and warm. Your spouse tells you that one of the children is not feeling well and asks you to go to the pharmacy to get some medicine. You gripe a little, but you are a good parent and agree to go. You get up, put on your winter coat, gloves, and stocking cap. As you go out the front door a blast of bitterly cold air hits you in the face. The car is very cold too, especially the seat.

When you arrive at the pharmacy, you see that only two parking places have been plowed out and that a single car is taking up both of them. You get out of your car and have to walk through knee-high snowdrifts to get inside. Quickly, what are your thoughts about the guy who took up two parking places?

Just as you go in, a man rushes past you as if you were not even there. You yell at him, "Ya jerk." But he doesn't even notice you. His eyes are glazed over. You approach the pharmacist and are about to grumble, when the pharmacist says, "The poor guy. His baby is dying. The doctor sent him here for some medicine, but it won't do any good. His baby will be dead by morning."

What are your thoughts now? "Boy I'm a jerk. I wish I hadn't said that."

What will you likely think if you pull into a pharmacy at some later date and someone is hogging the parking spaces? "I'm keeping my mouth shut. I'm not making that mistake again."

When something happens, we first tell ourselves what is going on, which in turn determines our emotions, which in turn directs our behavior.

What you think determines how you feel, which directs how you act.

When you thought that the guy who was hogging the parking spaces was a jerk, you had angry thoughts and did angry things. After you found out it was a terrible emergency, you felt overwhelming sorry for him and would have comforted him if you could have. The next time it happened you didn't jump to conclusions and felt calmer and more cautious.

Regardless of the response, it nevertheless was the same event each time. What made a difference in how you felt and acted was what you told yourself was going on.

It is our thoughts about events that determine how we feel and what we do, not the event. If you are in control of your thoughts, you will be in control of your feelings and what you do. We need to ask ourselves:

Is what I am thinking valid?

Do I really know what is going on?

Is it useful for me to feel and act the way I feel?

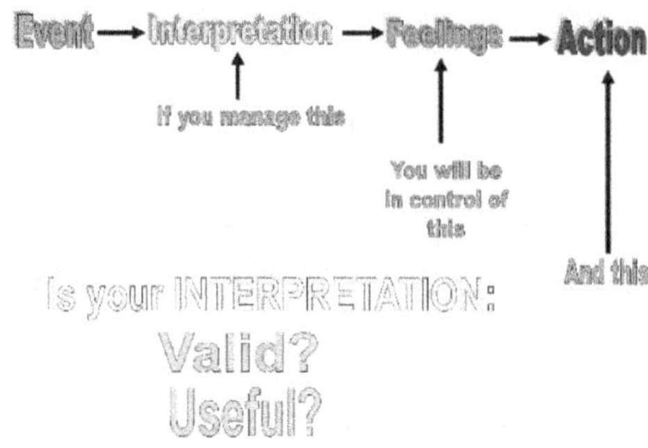

If it is not useful, then you should not act that way. We do not have to act the way we feel.

There are thoughts associated with these emotions.

Worry: I can't stand this. What should I do?"

Fear: "I can't take this. I've got to get away.

Sadness: This is awful and there's nothing I can do about it."

Anger: "He's not gonna get away with that."

These thoughts are often called automatic thoughts because they just flow. Often our actions just flow along with them, which may not always be in our best interest.

Sometimes these automatic thoughts are beliefs, sort of habits in the way we think. Imagine you were told from little on that:

> "You're stupid. You'll never amount to anything. I don't even know why you try."

If you are constantly being told something like that, either by others or yourself, that message will pop into your head and trigger your emotions. Since it is a habit, it occurs without thought, and you are seldom aware of it having occurred.

Imagine if your automatic thoughts change:

> "I'm not taking any crap off of anyone anymore."

You will be angry a lot and do angry stuff and get into lots of trouble.

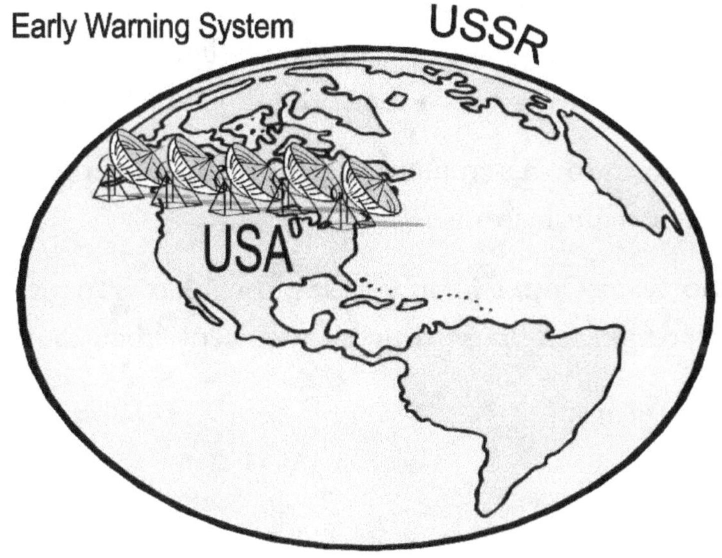

Now switching gears for a second. During the Cold War with the former Soviet Union, we built a series of radar stations along Alaska and northern Canada. They looked over the North Pole. If the Russians launched their bombers, our radar would pick that up. We would send up our bombers. Their radar would pick up our bombers and they would signal their planes to return to base. Then we would do the same. This early warning system averted many dangerous situations.

The reason that I am mentioning this is that we all have an early warning radar system in us that lets us know that a dangerous situation is just over the horizon.

You feel **sad, afraid, worried, or angry**. You will feel these emotions before you act on their urges.

When you feel these emotions, you need to take action.

1. **Shut up**: The first thing you do is shut up. When things are not going right, either our mouths are going a mile a minute, or our minds are. And you can't slow things down if you can't think.

2. **Take a step back**: Then you take a step back. The closer you are to the threatening situation, the stronger the fight or flight response. If you take a step back, it automatically slows down the feeling of threat and urgency.

3. **Take a deep breath**: Then take a deep breath. This too automatically slows down the fight or flight response.

4. **Problem-Solve or Cope**: Then you start problem-solving. Fix the problem. If it can't be fixed, then prepare yourself to accept what you cannot change.

Also, during the Cold War, we had air raid sirens everywhere. If the Russians did not turn around and an attack was imminent, the sirens would go off and we were all to go to our shelters until things were safe. The reason I bring that up is because we all have air raid sirens inside of us that let us know that an attack is imminent, and things are about to get out of hand.

We feel our hearts beat faster.

We begin to breathe faster.

We become tense.

Fight or Flight

1. Heart beats faster.
2. Breathing becomes faster.
3. Begin to sweat.
4. Blood is shunted to muscles.
5. Adrenaline is released.
6. Endorphenes are released.
7. Muscles tense.

If you feel these sensations, you need to give yourself a time out. Get away until you calm down. Then return to problem-solving in a calm manner.

Now on the piece of paper that you wrote your bad experience on. Read it and imagine how it might have turned out had you approached it with productive thoughts and productive emotions. Rewrite the story about how it would have happened if you had slowed down, and problem solved before you acted.

06 Darth Vader vs. Robert E. Lee

There are two groups of emotions:

Feel Bad Emotions

Feel Good Emotions

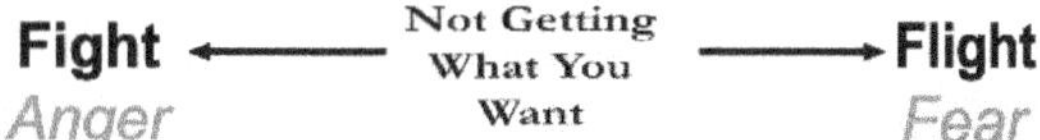

If the emotional mind has determined that something undesirable is about to happen, the brain prepares itself and the body to fight the threat or run away from it, the so-called "fight or flight response".

If the emotional mind decides to put a stop to the menace, it prepares to confront it with intimidation or force. This is experienced as anger or a related emotion.

If the emotional mind decides you cannot stop the menace, it prepares to run away. This is experienced as fear or a related emotion.

If the emotional mind senses an opportunity to get something it wants, a person will experience a feeling of either:

Power

Control

Elation

or Pleasure

Satisfaction

Joy

Power/control/elation are associated with mastery and the emotional urges to dominate a situation in order to obtain something of value. In contrast, pleasure/satisfaction/joy, among other things, are associated with a sense of well-being, security, and freedom from harm.

There is an old adage that you can get a donkey to do what you want with a carrot or a stick. Write the number 1 on a piece of paper and write then what you think that adage means?

In the movie *Star Wars*, the Rebels have stolen the plans to the Death Star and the Imperial Command is meeting to discuss getting them back. A dispute breaks out between Darth Vader and another commander. Darth Vader holds up his hand, conjuring up the Dark Side of the Force, and the commander grabs his throat as if he is being choked. All of the other commanders looked on in fright. Darth Vader releases the Dark Force and the commander's head drops to the table.

Write the number 2 on your piece of paper and then write why Darth Vader choked the man? Do you think that everyone else was intimidated by Darth Vader and the Dark Side of the Force? Will they all be less likely to cross Darth Vader in the future?

Of course, Darth Vader is just a fictional character. He does not exist. But, I believe, the Dark Side is very real and all around us.

A scene in the movie *9-5*, starring Dolly Parton, Lily Tomlin, and Jane Fonda shows this. Fonda's character is given a task on her first day on the job. She has to make copies on a big complex copy machine. It gets out of control, and she has papers flying everywhere. The boss, played by Dabney Coleman, comes in and begins to yell at her. "Any moron can operate this machine. You had better get it right or your first day will be your last." He didn't try to help her. He didn't try to teach her. He felt anger and tried to intimidate her to do things right. He felt powerful when he put her down.

"Any moron can operate that machine." That is the Dark Side, and it is very real

Write the number 3 on your paper and then write a sentence or two about someone that treated you that way.

This is a serious situation. Anger pushes you and power and control pulls you. Things happen double fast and with double strength.

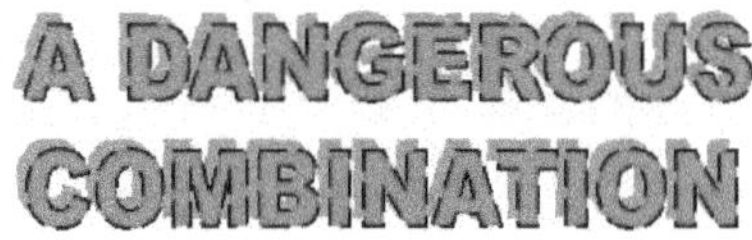

But there is another serious danger to the Dark Side.

In the *Return of the Jedi* Luke Skywalker was captured by Darth Vader and the Emperor was going to seduce him to the Dark Side. Do you remember how that was to happen? Write the number 4 down on your piece of paper and then your answer.

Darth Vader egged Luke into a fight so that he would get angry and lose control. The Emperor told Luke, "Your hate has made you powerful. Give yourself to the Dark Side." Luckily for Luke he remembered his Jedi training and did not go all the way into their mind trap.

Anger makes you feel bad. But getting your way, either in reality or just in your head, causes you to feel "powerful and in control." That makes you feel good. So, even though you might not want to feel angry, you might want to feel the power and control that can go with it. This gets you hooked on resentments.

When you hold a grudge, you won't problem solve or let things go, you will re-feel the anger (and feel bad) only to tell yourself how bad they are and how good you are. This makes you feel powerful and superior (and then you feel good). However, it's like an addiction. You need to do this all over and over again in order to feel good. Furthermore, it makes you feel as if any type of revenge is ok. You'll feel free to hurt other people and, as a result, have a life full of problems. But you have to make excuses to yourself why this is all ok.

"I don't like it when I hit my wife. But she shouldn't make me mad. And it's not like I beat her or anything."

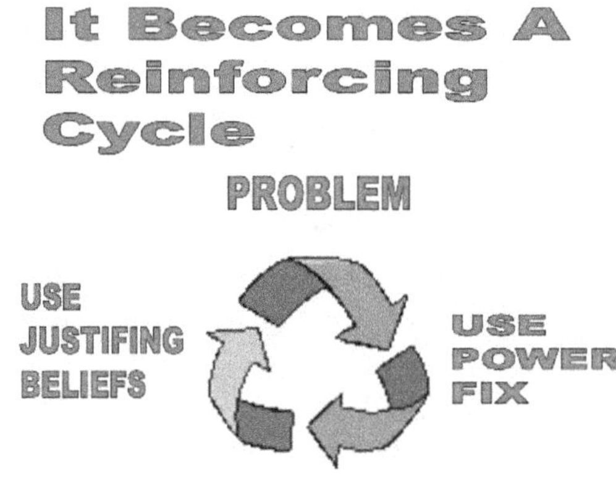

It becomes a vicious cycle. Something happens that you don't like, you get angry, use force or intimidation to get your way. You make excuses that it's okay, that makes you feel good and okay to do it again. However, force and intimidation tend to create more problems, so you've still got plenty of problems to feel angry about. And on it goes, getting worse and worse, until your life's a mess and so is everyone else's around you.

Here is an example of how a person's values may erode over time. The most important thing in this man's life is his daughter. He stops at a bar to use the phone. He leaves his daughter in the car. He is only going to be there for a minute. But he sees a friend and has a beer. He thinks "one won't hurt." But then he has another and another, forgetting his daughter. His wife gets angry at him when she finds out what he did.

He neglected his daughter and feels bad.

He could decide to be more caring and not do that again. If he keeps his word, he will feel better.

Or he might make an excuse for his behavior. "It's not like I robbed a bank or something. I don't know what the big deal is. No one's gonna tell me what to do." This too will make him feel better, but at a terrible price.

Over time these excuses erode a person's values.

Making excuses so you can feel good and still do harmful things.

Here are some ways that people can make excuses (Adapted from Albert Bandura):

Moral Justification: Bad behavior is excused by reframing it as a social or moral good. For example, it's all right to miss the kids' game in order to get ahead at work.

Euphemistic Language: Bad behavior is made to feel less so by using language that minimizes the harm done. For example, "It is all right to call them names when I am just teaching them a lesson. "

Advantageous Comparison: The belief of having done something wrong is minimized by comparing oneself with others who are doing worse things. For example, "I just left the kid in the car for a while. It's not like I robbed a bank or something."

Displacement of Responsibility: The belief of having done something wrong is minimized when it is viewed as has having a cause outside of your control. For example, "You can't blame me. That's just the way I was raised. I can't help myself."

Diffusion of Responsibility: The belief of having done something wrong is minimized by spreading the blame among many other people. For example, "You can't blame me. Everyone else does it."

Distorting Consequences: Harmful behavior is minimized by disregarding or reducing the belief about the harm done. For example, "The kids weren't really hurt that much anyway."

Attribution of Blame: Bad behavior is dissipated when a person blames someone else for having given them no choice for their behavior. For example, "I wouldn't have hit him if he hadn't made me angry. "

Dehumanization: The belief of having done something wrong is dissipated if you see the victim as less than human. For example, "Stupid bitch."

Pick the three neutralizing thoughts that you believe cause the most harm. Then write the number 5 on your paper, write your choices, and why you picked them.

If you use these justifications, they become thinking habits that erode your values and spread into all other areas of your life.

Yoda, the Jedi Master, said, "Once you start down the dark path, forever will it dominate your destiny. Consume you it will."

However, there is a way to avoid the Dark Side:

Controlling your anger.

Letting go of resentments.

Problem-solving

Cooperation

A WAY OUT OF THE DARK SIDE

These are effective means of getting what you want without creating more problems - and they feel good too.

Let us finish with a scene from the movie *Gettysburg*. This is an example of when things can go better when cooperation is the theme. In July 1863, General Lee with 70,000 men marched into Pennsylvania where they accidentally bumped into 90,000 Union forces in the small town of Gettysburg. The Union held the high ground after the first day of fighting, giving them the advantage. The reason that they just bumped into each other is that the Confederate General, J.E.B. Stewart, didn't do his job right. His mission was to ride around with his cavalry forces, locate the enemy and size up the lay of the land. Had he done this, General Lee would have chosen the location of the battle and forced the Union to attack him at their disadvantage. Now General Lee must reprimand General Stewart. He has every right to be angry. He certainly has the power. How does he handle it?

Lee starts out by explaining to Stewart that his duty was to determine the enemy's movements and the lay of the land. Then report back. Lee tells him that he failed in his duty. He tells him that it must "never, never happen again." Stewart becomes upset and offers his resignation. Lee starts to get angry but composes himself. He takes a step back and then a deep breath and then tells Stewart, "There has been a mistake. It will not happen again. You are one of the finest cavalry officers I have ever known and your service to this army is invaluable. Now, let us speak no more of this."

"There has been a mistake. It will not happen again. I know your quality. You are one of the finest officers I have ever known." Contrast that with: "Any moron can operate this machine (what the manager said in the movie 9-5)." General Lee could have gotten mad. In fact, he did. But he took a deep breath and calmed down. He wanted to make Stewart a more valuable officer. If General Lee had belittled Stewart, Lee might have felt powerful, but Stewart would have felt bad and would not have been encouraged to do better. Instead, General Stewart left with a greater sense of mission and went on to fight gallantly for his cause.

Think of a time when someone helped you rather than treated you badly.

Write the number 6 on your paper and then write about your experience. Add why you think this was a better way to do things.

07 Problem-Solving

One of the scenes from the movie *The Peacemaker*, starring George Clooney and Nicole Kidman, shows an old Russian farmer out in his backyard when a military train rushes by. He goes into his house and a short time later hears a terrible crash. The old man and his wife go out to investigate. Shortly afterwards a nuclear explosion engulfs them.

The scene then switches to Washington D.C. where intelligence personnel are studying the data from the explosion. Since they think that a train accident caused an unintended nuclear detonation, the United States would not be threatened. We would have monitored fallout, as well as sent environmental and medical experts to help.

Then the character played by Kidman discovers that it could not have been an accident. She believes that it was a terrorist act. Some group had a gripe against Russia and set the bomb off in an attempt to force political changes. Again, we would probably still monitor fallout and send medical help. We would also offer what knowledge we had on terrorists who had a gripe against Russia. However, we would not feel too threatened.

Then at a debriefing, Clooney's character rather brazenly takes over. He points to pictures of the train collision and shows that no one had jumped off the train carrying the nukes, while people were jumping off the other train. He concludes that someone killed all of the people on the nuke train and stole several nuclear bombs. The explosion was just to throw everyone off track. Suddenly, the United States was in a threatening situation. Many people would like to get their hands on a nuclear bomb and explode one in the United States.

In fact, that is the plot. A Bosnian terrorist has bought one of the bombs and plans to blow it up in downtown Manhattan on Friday during rush hour, killing millions of people. Suddenly the problem to be solved is tracking down the thieves and getting our hands on the bombs. If they had focused their problem-solving on the environmental and humanitarian issues, as they did at first, many Americans would have died. Using our problem-solving skills correctly is very important not only for anti-terrorist forces, but for everyday people.

Some people might think that they do all right with problem-solving. "My life is not that complicated. I don't have to chase terrorists." Maybe so but let me ask you something. Are you a parent? Are you worried about your children being kidnapped by strangers? A solution many people take for this problem is to drive their kids to and from school.

Well, the reality is that kidnappings by strangers are very rare. 95% of all missing children are runaways. The other 5% is almost all kidnappings by noncustodial parents. Kidnappings by strangers are very rare. In a small town of 30,000 people, if they had one missing kid a week, which would be a lot, it would be 100 years between kidnappings by strangers. We know about kidnappings when they happen because it makes all the papers. Nevertheless, most parents would rather be safe than sorry. We wouldn't want our child to be that statistic.

Have you ever been by a middle school when it lets out? There are cars two and three layers deep, all jockeying for position. Kids are weaving in and out of all this trying to get to their cars. You can be sure that more kids are hurt or killed by our solution to the kidnapping problem than will ever be hurt by kidnappers. So, we really do have to take a good look at how we solve problems if we want our lives to go well.

If you remember, the way the emotional mind makes decisions and solves problems is by automatically telling us:

This is what is going on.

This is what I should do about it.

There is no thinking. There are no choices, things just flow. The emotional mind solves short-term, surface problems without consideration for anything else that may be important to you.

On the other hand, your thinking mind makes decisions by asking:

1. What is really going on?

2. What are my options?

3. What is the best deal under the circumstances?

We will be studying problem-solving using your thinking mind and how to keep your emotional mind from interfering.

The first step in this problem-solving skill is to ask, "What is really going on?" You'll remember that your emotional mind automatically tells you what is going on. But it doesn't always get things right.

There are three sub-steps to figuring out what is really going on that will help you be more accurate:

How do you know when you have a problem?

How to identify the main problem?

How to separate facts from assumptions.

"What do you mean? I know when I have a problem. I don't need to mess around thinking about it." Ok, let me tell you something that evil scientists found out.

If you take a frog, put it in a pot of water and then put the pot on a hot stove, the frog will boil to death. By the time the frog's little brain realizes that it is in trouble, its system is already paralyzed, and it cannot jump out.

People sometimes act like frogs. We wait until we are in hot water before we decide we need to act. In other words, we wait until our problems are bad before we recognize that we need to do something. It is much easier to take care of things early before they get bad. But how do we know early on that a problem is brewing? Write the number 1 on a piece of paper and then write how you know when you have a problem.

One way we know when we have a problem is that we feel:

    angry

    anxious

    fearful

    sad

If we learn to pay attention to how we feel, we can jump in when we first recognize we have a problem rather than wait until it gets out of hand.

Next, we need to identify the main problem. Rather than explain what this means, let me give an example.

Imagine you went to college and got a degree in, let's say, computer programming. You did well and had high hopes. Then you found out there were no jobs for computer programmers in your town and you ended up working at a minimum wage job. You are really bummed out. Then one day you saw an ad for a programmer at the local plant. It pays really good. You called them up and told them your qualifications. They said you were a good candidate and set you an appointment. On the way there, your car broke down. Write the number 2 on your paper and then write what the problem is.

If you thought the problem was that your car was broken, you would have focused on fixing your car. In reality, you want to fix your car so you can get to the interview on time. Fixing your car is only one option for getting to the interview on time. Your emotional mind is short-term focused, and you have to deliberately look at the big picture for good problem-solving. If you fix the car, you might get to the interview on time, but be a mess. Or you might fix it but be late. Or you might not be able to fix it at all.

If you focus on how to get to the interview on time, you might come up with options that will accomplish your goal and do not have these drawbacks. So, when you have a problem, ask yourself what is really important here and focus on solving that.

The next step is gathering facts. It has three sub-steps:

Careful observations

Asking the right questions

Separating facts from assumptions.

In the movie, only George Clooney looks at the pictures close enough to notice that no one was jumping off the train carrying the nukes. Your emotional mind sees what it thinks is there, not always what is really there. The good problem solver takes a second and a third systematic look at things to decide what is really going on.

At first glance, these two pictures are the same, but a close look shows 11 differences.

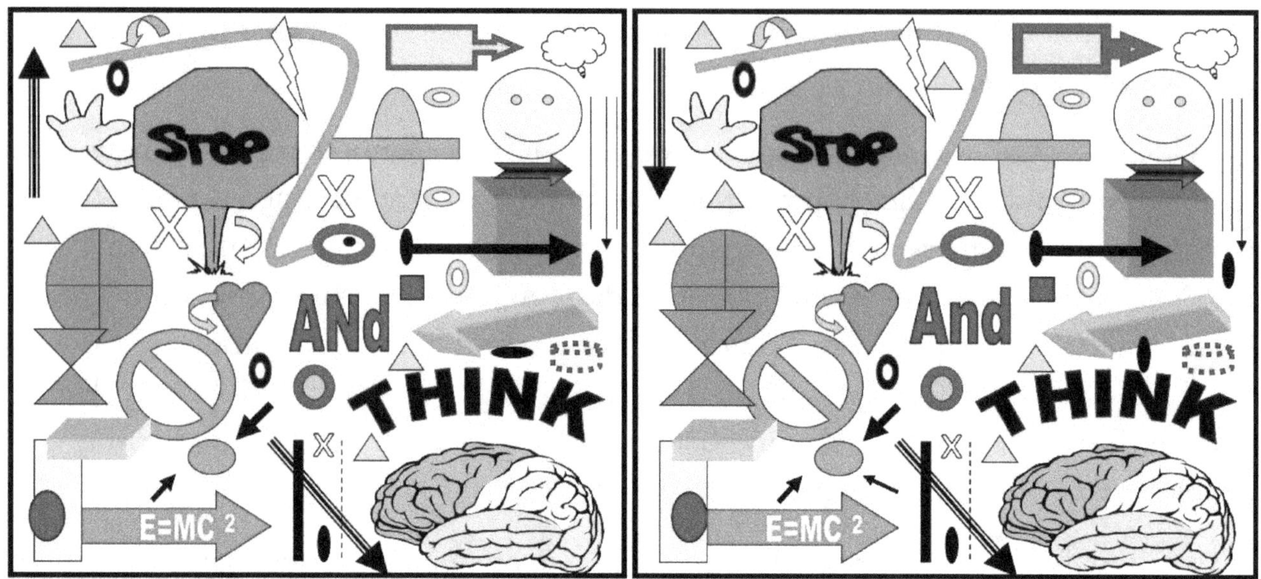

What are they? Write the number 3 on your paper and then list the differences.

Here are the differences looking with the picture on the left:

1) arrow on upper left points up

2) triangle near lightning in upper center missing

3) arrows in lines on upper right is in the middle

4) lasso with loop in middle has a dot in it

5) arrow to right of lasso loop is longer

6) the N in the word "and" is capitalized

7) hourglass on lower left is smaller

8) oval in block on lower left is on left side of block

9) arrow pointing to oval in center bottom is missing

10) oval above the word "think" is horizontal

11) box with arrow, at the top center, has a thinner boarder.

Your next step is to ask the right questions. Remember, ask the person who is most likely to have the correct information. Don't ask your plumber about a heart problem or your doctor about problems with your pipes.

Now let me tell you a story:

Melissa's dead naked body lay on the floor. She is in a puddle of water. The window is open, and the breeze is blowing the curtains about. There is broken glass everywhere. What happened to Melissa?

Write the number 4 on your paper and write what questions you would ask to get the answer.

Melissa was a fish. The wind blew over her fishbowl and it broke on the floor. She suffocated.

Most of the time people make guesses about what happened rather than ask questions that gather information. That's the way the emotional mind works. It jumps from idea to idea in a hurry. It doesn't like to go slow and systematically.

Next, we will do another story and ask specific fact-finding questions.

Did you take journalism in school? Write the number 5 on your paper and then write the specific questions reporters are taught to ask.

Write the number 6 on your paper and then write down some: who, what, where, when, why, and how questions that might fill us in on the story of this newspaper article.

MUSCATINE 01/05/99 A Pennsylvania man accused of transporting more than 100 pounds of marijuana will be arraigned on drug charges later this month. John Doe, 44, of Hermitage, Pa., is charged with possession of a controlled substance with the intent to deliver. Doe was arrested during a routine traffic stop near Wilton Monday after the Iowa State Patrol found 141 pounds of marijuana in his car. If convicted, Doe faces up to 10 years in prison on the possession charge.

Would answers to your "who, what, when, why, and how" questions have given you the gist of the story?

The next step is for you to separate facts from assumptions.

Imagine you are a schoolteacher. You walk out onto the playground and find two kids fighting. One is black and one is white. If you think to yourself, "Why is that black kid picking on the white kid?" You would be making a racist assumption that black people are troublemakers. On the other hand, you might think, "why is that white kid picking on the black kid?" This is also a racist assumption. It assumes that white people are racists and go out of their way to harm black people. Either way, the assumptions will color your judgment and get in the way of finding out what actually happened.

Write the number 7 on your paper and then write the known facts of this story?

The only facts we have so far are that two kids are fighting in the playground; one is black, and one is white. Any other ideas are assumptions.

By the way, did you think in your mind that the two kids that were fighting were boys? Most people assume that, but that was not stated.

Study this picture. Write the number 8 on your paper and then write facts about it. Don't make any assumptions.

The man on the left has a prosthesis (an artificial arm).

He is black. Is he an African American? We don't know. He could be French.

He is wearing an Army shirt. Was he in the Army? We don't know. Anyone can buy a used army shirt.

Is his name Franks? We don't know. He may have borrowed it from Franks.

The little black girl is holding his hand. What is their relationship? We don't know. He could be her father, brother or even babysitter.

She is wearing bibs.

There is a little girl in the lower right-hand corner holding a doll.

The older man has glasses on. Is he old? Old is relative.

He has on what some call an overseas cap. Was he in the military? We don't know.

He has a bow tie and a jacket on.

Are the two men saluting? This is really technical, but we don't know. To salute you have to be saluting at something and we cannot see that they are. The best we can say is that they have their hands to their foreheads in a saluting position.

Are they at a parade? We don't know.

There is a lawn chair behind the black girl.

There is the number 8 and some balloons behind the older man.

Your emotional mind assumes that what it decides is fact and then doesn't continue to check things out. It often ignores evidence that is inconsistent with its assumptions. That is why it is so important to make yourself take a second or third check on what you think is really the situation.

It is impossible to gather all of the facts. Sometimes you have to work with assumptions, but at least label them as such in your mind so that you are not blinded by them and ignore the possibility that they might be wrong.

After you've got a good handle on what is really going on, you need to give yourself some options. Your emotional mind does not give you options. It automatically tells you what is going on and automatically tells you what to do about it. Your thinking mind, however, is creative. It can think of many things you can do, and you can pick from them to get the best deal under the circumstances.

There are two sub-steps for coming up with your options:

1. Brainstorming

2. Short-term and long-tern consequential thinking

Brainstorming is a way to take advantage of your creativity. But let's do something before we get into that.

Are you hungry? Following is a menu. Figure out what you want to eat. Write the number 9 on your paper and then place your order.

Food R Us

Buffalo Wings.....................order of 12......$4.99	Pizza...........1 topping.............small............$6.85
Breadsticks.........................order of 5..........$1.80	medium...........$9.95
order of 10......$2.99	large.....…......$12.15
extra sauce......$ .85	additional toppings:
Garlic Bread.......................order of 2.…......$ .95	small...$ .90 each
with cheese......$1.20	medium..$1.10 each
order of 4.…......$1.60	large...$1.35 each
with cheese......$2.40	Toppings: Pepperoni Sausage Hamburger Ham
Salad Bar...........................with a meal...…...$2.80	Mushrooms Onions Olives Green Peppers
as a meal........$3.45	Spaghetti....................................…...........$3.85
Soft Drinks..........................glass.…...…......$ .99	with meat sauce $4.50
pitcher..........$2.90	Lasagna....................................….........$4.75
Beer................................glass....…........$1.30	
pitcher..........$4.90	
Coffee/Tea...........................glass....…......$ .60	

A lot of people study the menu, look at all of the choices and then order. Surprisingly, however, many people tackle problems by thinking of possible solutions, evaluating each solution as they came up with them and then stopping once they come up with an idea that seems good.

This approach would be like reading the menu and stopping at Buffalo Wings because you like Buffalo Wings, then later kicking yourself when you found out that you could have had pepperoni pizza instead. And you love pepperoni pizza more than anything. You wished you had read the whole menu before you ordered.

If you are trying to come up with ideas, just come up with ideas. Do not evaluate them until later. Stopping to evaluate as you go disrupts creativity and tempts you to stop before you have explored the options thoroughly. You can evaluate your ideas later, but at first just brainstorm.

There is one more thing you should know about brainstorming before you try it. Think of the names of five family members, friends, or acquaintances.

Write the number 10 on your paper and then write their first names.

Write five more names.

Five more.

After you came up with the first few names, you probably thought you were out of names. However, if you kept at it, you came up with more. You tapped into your creativity. Do not give up when you first run out of ideas while brainstorming. Keep at it, even if it seems silly. New and creative ideas are just waiting to pop out if you stick with it.

Now, think back to the job interview and the broken car problem. Brainstorm "How can I make it to the interview on time?" Remember, just come up with ideas. Do not stop to think if they are good or bad. Write the number 11 on your paper and then write them down, even if they seem silly.

Here is a list some brainstormers came up with.

    fix the car

    take a cab

hitchhike

call a friend

call an enemy

run

walk

steal a bike

steal a car

hop

skip

jump

use a pogo stick

take a plane

take a bus

take a jet

ask somebody to carry you

call 911

call the interviewer and tell him you will be late

 call a tow truck

ask people on the street for help

stand on the corner and hope the interviewer walks by

take the subway

take a train

take a boat

fax the interviewer

e-mail the interviewer

have Scotty beam you there

borrow a horse

steal a horse

buy a horse

buy a car

buy a bike

pray

make an animal sacrifice

call your minister

call your mom

call your dad

call your brother

call your sister

call your wife

call your ex-wife

call a doctor

wish yourself there

ask a cop for help

call your mechanic

call AAA

call AA

call an old drinking friend

call one of your coworkers

Many of these are just plain stupid. But some of them are good. We might have missed some of the good ones if we had just stopped with "fix the car."

After you've got your list, cross off the dumb ones.

Now we're ready to do some long term-short term consequential thinking. While some ideas might solve the problem in the short term, they can cause problems over time.

For example, you might have gotten to the interview on time if you had stolen a car. But what good would all of that be if you were shortly thereafter sent to prison?

A good real-life example is what happened to Australia. In the late 1600's the British colonized Australia. They set up huge plantations and were getting rich. But the English gentlemen were bored. Back home they liked to fox hunt and shooting kangaroos didn't seem cricket. They brought over some rabbits for hunting and food. They solved their problem in the short run.

Unfortunately, there were no natural predatory enemies for rabbits in Australia, so they bred and bred until their numbers nearly destroyed the economy. In the long run, their solution was disastrous. Today's solutions should not become tomorrow's problems. And they won't be, if we stop and think of the consequences before we decide what to do.

The last step is to figure out what is the best deal under the circumstances.

Most people think they know what they want and often they do. However, approaching this question carefully makes sure that you do not skip anything before you decide what you want to do.

You can do this with two thinking skills:

1. Considering Other People

2. Pluses & Minuses

Most of the problems you face involve other people. You might think a good plan would make other people's views unimportant. After all, a good plan is a good plan. However, people think, feel, and want differently than each other, and if you want to get other people to cooperate, on this and other problems, you have to add that to your plan.

In the extreme, a bad solution might create enemies that will sabotage you now and even later on. For example, if your car broke down on the way to an interview, one possible solution is to call your brother. He could come and give you a ride. That would certainly solve your problem. However, it is 1 PM and he works nights. This is the middle of his sleeping time. He might help, but he might also feel he was being pestered. Maybe another solution might work just as well and not create new problems.

The last thinking tool is Pluses and Minuses. It is easy to get stuck on a solution that you like and only think of why it is good. It is just as easy to reject an idea that you do not like and only look at the negative side. Doing Pluses and Minuses forces you to intentionally look at both the good side and the bad side. Pluses and Minuses keeps you from deciding the value of an idea based on your initial feelings rather than on the value of the idea.

After you look at both sides of the issue, your original feelings might be the same. Then again, they might have changed. You would never have known which position was best if you had just stopped thinking after your initial thoughts.

Let's try this with marijuana. Write the number 12 on your paper and then write 5 reasons marijuana should be legalized and 5 reasons why it should not. The idea is to think about both sides of the issue whether you agree with the other side or not.

Now it is a simple step to look over the choices and pick the one that has the most to gain at the least costs.

You might be thinking that careful problem-solving is ok, "but who has time to go through all of this?" Or maybe you are thinking, "this is just too much work."

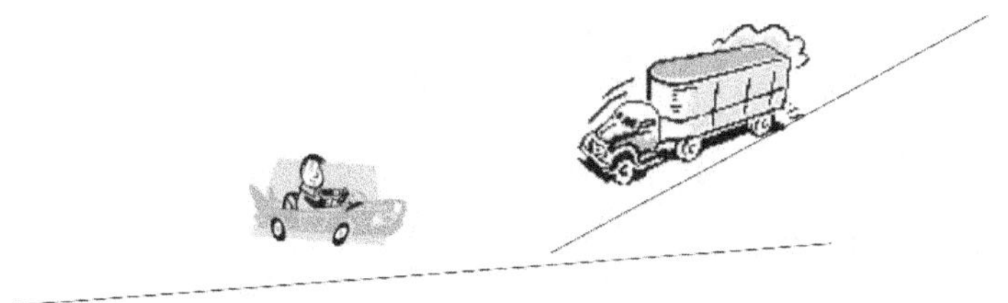

If a truck is zooming at you 70 miles per hour, you don't have time to stop and ask yourself, "Hey, what is really going on here?" You do not have time to do all of this problem-solving. You are better off relying on your gut reactions under these circumstances. But how many times a day do you have to make split-second decisions concerning important matters? How much time do you have to make most of the decisions you face daily? Few of your problems really require split-second decisions. Most of the time we have minutes, hours, and days to make decisions.

Write the number 13 on your paper and write about something that happened in your life that would have turned out better if you had done just a little of this problem-solving first before you acted.

1. What is really going on?

A. How do you know when you have a problem.

B. How to identify the main problem.

C. How to gather the facts.

1. Careful Observation
2. Asking the Right Questions
3. Seperating Facts from Assumptions

2. What are my choices?

A. Brainstorming

B. Short term and long term consequential thinking

3. What is the best deal under the circumstances?

A. Considering Other People

B. Pluses & Minuses

08 Being Responsible

In the movie *The Blues Brothers* the characters played by Dan Aykroyd and John Belushi are being shot at by the character played by Carrie Fisher. Belushi stood Fisher up at the church on their wedding day and she is going to get her revenge by killing him.

However, he begs her not to do it. Then he tells her, "I ran out of gas. I had a flat tire. I didn't have enough money for the cab fare. My tux didn't come back from the cleaners. An old friend came in from out of town. Someone stole my car. There was an earthquake. A terrible flood. Locusts. It wasn't my fault."

She softens and forgives him.

Write the number 1 on a piece of paper and then answer whether you think there really was a flood, locusts, and earthquakes? Or did he just say those things to get out of a jam?

Write the number 2 on your paper and then write how you think it hurts a person, in the long run, when they knowingly make excuses for things they have done that hurt other people?

You are going to read two stories and then do an activity. The two stories are stupid - so don't say they are stupid, because you have already been told that they are.

A man was walking down the street, and a piano fell on his head.

Yeah, yeah. That was stupid. It wasn't a good story either.

Now for a second story:

A guy was driving down the highway and a train pulled along beside him. He raced it to the crossing, tried to beat it, but didn't make it.

Now for the activity. Write the number 3 down on your paper. Then write what this is a picture of.

Now write the number 4 down on your paper. Then write what this is a picture of.

Some people see a picture of an old woman. Others see a picture of a young woman. Can you see both the young woman and the old woman?

Most people, if they see the above picture of an old woman, see an old woman when they look at the picture on the right.

If, however, they had been shown the above picture of a young woman first, they probably would have seen a young woman when they looked at the picture on the left.

If you study this picture for a while, you will see both an old woman and a young woman. Whichever picture a person sees first (young woman or old woman) conditions them to see this picture as being similar. It's as if our earlier experiences shape the way we think about later experiences.

Following are some terms. Think about how they relate to the two stories we just read and the young/old woman picture.

> **Fate** refers to things that happen to us that we had no part in causing. We have no choice. For example, you did not pick your race.
>
> **Nature** refers to things you do because you like to do them that way. For example, you like to dive off the high board at the swimming pool, because you like excitement.
>
> **Nurture** relates to things you do because you were raised to do them. For example, your dad taught you to help people in need, so you do.

Write the number 5 on your paper and then match each definition to the story or set of pictures that fits best.

As a rule, most people pick the piano falling on the guy's head as fate, because it was not something that he had a part in causing. It just happened to him. He had no choice.

Most people pick the train wreck for nature because the guy likes to take chances, and he took a chance and lost. He chooses excitement.

Sometimes people pick the train wreck as nurture because they were raised to take chances. Maybe, but most people who like to take risks choose to do so because they like fun and excitement, not because of how they are raised.

Most people have a little harder time with nurture, because this example doesn't always jump out at them, but the old woman/young woman is like nurture. When a person saw either the young woman picture or saw the old woman picture, it taught them to see the third picture as being similar to the original picture they looked at. Life is like that. If you were raised in a family to act a certain way, acting that way sort of just happens. If you were raised in a family to act a different way, then acting that way just sort of happens.

However, and this is a big however, just as the third picture was not an old woman or a young woman, but both; neither is the world all one way or all another. It is a bunch of ways. You are not stuck acting the way you were brought up. If you think about different ways of acting, you can choose to act differently than the way you were raised – if that works out better.

Here are some life situations:

    a. I have parents that are alcoholics.

    b. I go drinking every Friday and Saturday night.

    c. I smoke pot every chance I get.

    d. I have a dad that used to beat me.

    e. I am on probation.

    f. I have a good job.

    g. I have a bad job.

    h. I hang out in bars.

If fate means things that happen to us that we had no part in causing, we had no choice, which of these life situations happened because of fate? Write the number 6 on your paper and then your answers.

a. I have parents that are alcoholics. You don't pick your parents, so that would be fate.

b. I go drinking every Friday and Saturday night. You might like to go drinking every weekend or you might have been raised that way, but it is something you choose to do, so it is not fate.

c. I smoke pot every chance I get. You may like to smoke pot or were raised around people who smoked pot, but you have control over whether you do it or not. So, it's not fate.

d. I have a dad that used to beat me. You do not control another person's behavior. You might or might not have done something for which your dad chooses to beat you, but he chooses to do it, not you. This is fate in that sense.

e. I am on probation. The judge chose to put you on probation. But you chose to act in the way that got you in trouble. This is not fate in that sense.

f. I have a good job. You may have a good work history and have developed the needed skills. In that sense this is not fate. However, you might have just been lucky to be in the right place at the right time to get a job. That would be fate.

g. I have a bad job. You may have a poor work history and never developed the needed skills. In that sense this is not fate. However, you might have just been unlucky and there were no good jobs at the time. That would be fate.

h. I hang out in bars. You might just like to hang out in bars, or you might have been raised that way, but it is something you choose to do, so it is not fate.

Write the number 7 on your paper and then list at least 5 things that happened to you that were just fate, 5 things that you do just because of your nature, because you like to do those things, and 5 things that you do because you were brought up that way.

Write the number 8 on your paper and then think about the act that you did that got you in trouble. Was it fate, nature, or nurture? Write your answer down.

Write the number 9 on your paper and then think about whether a person can choose to act differently from the way that they like to act or can act differently than the way they were brought up. Can they sometimes overcome fate? Write your thoughts on the paper.

Write the number 10 on your paper and then write how it hurts a person, in the long run, if they blame their fate, their nature, or the way they were brought up for the harm they cause others, rather than problem-solving (fix things) or cope (accept what they cannot change)?

Write the number 11 on your paper and then write what happens to a person if they tell themselves that they cannot change.

09 The Callous Heart

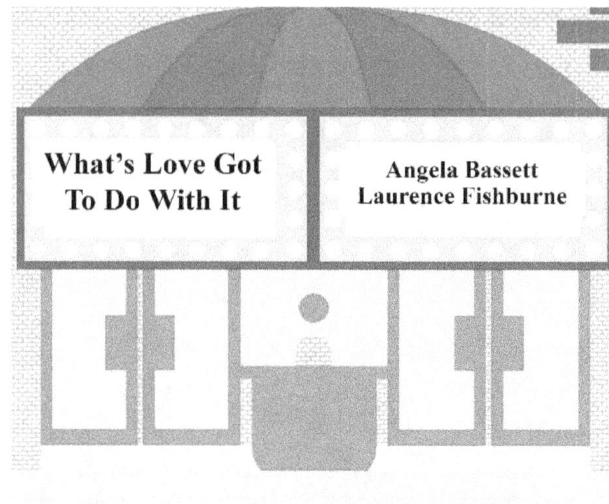

In the movie *What's Love Got to Do With It*, the rock star Tina Turner had just been beaten up by her husband, Ike Turner. She decided that she had to leave him before he kills her.

She runs across the street, dodging cars right and left. She runs into another motel. Her face is covered in blood. She tells the manager that she had just had a fight with her husband and doesn't have any money on her, but if he gave her a room, she promised that she would pay him back. The manager looks her over. His face is full of emotion. He says, "Don't worry. We'll take care of you."

Write the number 1 on a piece of paper and then answer these questions. What emotion do you think the motel manager was experiencing? Did he have to help her? Why did he want to take care of her?

He was probably feeling compassion and sorrow. While he didn't have to help, he probably did because she needed help, and it was the right thing to do.

Now, let's discuss the movie *Schindler's List*. The scene we are considering takes place in a Nazi concentration camp during World War II. The Nazis arrested Jews just because of their religion and put them in prison. A young Jewish woman is being forced to help assemble a building for the Nazis. She is a college-educated engineer.

The young woman is telling the workers that they need to do something differently. The commandant says that they are not going to take orders from Jews and orders that she be shot on the spot.

A German officer takes her to the side, pushes her to a kneeling position, puts a pistol to the back of her head and shoots her dead.

It takes but a minute from the commandant's order until her life is over.

The German officer walks away from the body with no expression on his face and rejoins the commandant. Their conversation picks up where they had left off before the murder was committed.

Write the number 2 on your paper and then write what emotion you think the German officer might have been feeling?

It was probably nothing. No feeling. It wasn't anger. Anger has a special look on a person's face. He had no expression. He might just as easily have been swatting a fly, but even that leaves a look of annoyance on one's face. There was no feeling at all.

The Hotel manager felt empathy. He could sense how other people felt and had feelings for them. In this case he felt sorry for Tina Turner and that sorrow stirred compassion in him. He wanted to help her.

The opposite of empathy is indifference, feeling nothing for others. The German officer could not feel the young woman's fear and pain, nor the tragedy of a life cut short. The violence meant nothing to him

Take out another piece of paper and make a chart like this:

EMPATHY (feeling for others)

1.

2.

3.

4.

5.

6.

7.

8.

9.

10.

INDIFFERENCE (lack of empathy)

Then think about where you might fall on this chart and circle the number.

Now for something a little different. Write the number 3 on your other paper and then answer these questions: Have you ever done hard work with your hands? Did you ever develop calluses? What are calluses?

When you do hard work, your hands get hurt some. Your body protects you from future pain by making your skin thicker. The thick skin is the callous and it lets you keep on doing the hard work without pain.

Now imagine what it would feel like to rub your hand on something soft, like a kitty and then on something rough, like a piece of sandpaper. The soft thing feels good and the sandpaper hurts.

Now imagine what it would feel like if you rubbed a piece of sandpaper wearing a thick pair of gloves. Like a callous, the glove would protect your hand. It wouldn't hurt.

Now imagine what it would feel like to stroke the kitty wearing the thick gloves. While the thick glove protects you from feeling bad, it also keeps you from feeling good things as well.

Do you think the German officer was always so cold blooded? Do you think that long before the war he loved, laughed, cared for other people, and had other people who truly cared for him? Before the war, do you think he might have been horrified if he had seen someone shot before his eyes? Write the number 4 on your piece of paper and then write your thoughts on this.

He probably was not always so cold blooded, so calloused. At one time, he probably experienced lots of the feel-good emotions and would have been horrified to have witnessed a cold-blooded murder, let alone commit one.

How does someone go from a decent person, like the manager at the motel, to one who is so uncaring, so callous, so indifferent to someone else's suffering? Write the number 5 on your piece of paper and then your thoughts on this.

When the German Officer first did something that he thought was wrong, it was probably not something terrible, but he felt bad about hurting the other person. However, rather than allowing himself to feel bad, to feel remorse or be sorry, he somehow talked himself into thinking that under the circumstances what he did was okay. He told himself things like, "Jews aren't human." or "I'm only following orders." or "If I didn't do it, someone else would have."

Just like the calluses on your hands, he added layers of beliefs that protected him from the pain and allowed him to continue doing what was wrong.

The thicker the layers, the easier it was to do worse and worse things. The callused heart not only protected him from bad feelings, however, but prevented him from feeling good emotions too. He lost the ability to feel pain and also to love, to laugh and to care for other people. Eventually, he didn't care about anything (good or bad), and nobody cared for him much either.

You'll remember from a few lessons back that what you think determines how you feel, which directs how you act. People can tell themselves things that allow them to commit crimes and then convince themselves that it was unavoidable or okay for some reason. That prevents them from feeling bad, but also leads to a callused heart (hurting themselves and everyone around them).

Here are some "Indifferent Thoughts" that cause harm:

1. They deserved it.

2. No one was really hurt that much anyway.

3. She's making too big a deal over this.

4. It's a tough world and I ain't any worse than anyone else.

5. It ain't my fault.

6. I was high.

7. I was just teaching her about sex.

8. They made me mad.

9. I didn't have a choice.

10. I really did them a favor.

11. If I hadn't done it, someone else would have.

12. They knew better than to do that to me.

13. It's a stupid law anyway.

14. Everyone else is doing it.

15. I didn't really want that to happen.

16. I was drunk.

17. They've got insurance, so no one was hurt.

18. Everyone is really crooked anyway.

19. I'm no worse than anyone else.

20. They screwed me, I screwed them back.

21. I don't want to think about it.

22. Screw everybody.

23. (Your idea)__________________.

24. (Your idea)__________________.

Pick the five excuses that you think have allowed the worst things to happen in the world. Write the number 6 on your paper and then write the five you picked.

EMPATHY (feeling for others)
1.
2.
3.
4.
5.
6.
7.
8.
9.
10.
INDIFFERENCE (lack of empathy)

Now write the excuses that you have used before on the left side of your other paper, the one with empathy on the top and indifference on the bottom.

Look at the "indifferent thoughts" that you wrote on the left side of your other paper, the one with empathy on the top and indifference on the bottom. Re-write those thoughts (on the right side of the paper) so that it makes you more sensitive to other people's feelings, which aren't excuses, that hold yourself accountable for what you do, but also keep you from getting a callous heart.

Now write the number 7 on your other piece of paper and then write the advantages of not thinking callous thoughts.

10 The Cost Of Living With Crime

Let's see just how good you are at handling money. We will have a contest.

CONTEST

Write the number 1 on a piece of paper. Then write $1000 and draw a car or truck next to the number.

You live in a high crime area. There is a lot of vandalism and theft going on. You can:

   A. Not buy insurance and take your chances (no cost)

   B. Buy $200 deductible for $100 (if your vehicle is vandalized or stolen the insurance will pay anything above $200)

   C. Buy non-deductible for $300 (if your vehicle is vandalized or stolen the insurance will pay all damages)

There are 3 other rules:

1. If your vehicle is damaged, you have to fix it, if you have the money. If you cannot afford it, you must borrow the money.

2. If your vehicle is stolen, you have to buy another of equal value if you have the money. If you cannot afford it, you must borrow the money.

3. If you have to borrow money to get something fixed or replaced, you will have to write "BORROWED" and the amount on your paper.

Write the number 2 on your paper. Then pick your insurance policy and write its letter (A, B or C) on your paper. Then subtract the cost of that policy from your $1000 and write the answer on your paper. (If math is not one of your strong points you may need to ask for help.)

Here is your policy.

While you were all sleeping, without a care in the world, a bunch of people were partying. They got drunk and swept through your area vandalizing and stealing vehicles. When you woke up, you saw what they had done.

Write the number 3 on your piece of paper and then randomly pick the Roman Numeral I or II or III or IV and write it down.

If you wrote I, your tires were slit - $200 damage:

- If you had no insurance (insurance choice A) - deduct $200 from what is left of your money.

- If you had $200 deductible (insurance choice B)- deduct $200 from what is left of your money.

- If you had non-deductible (insurance choice C) - your insurance pays for repairs.

If you wrote II, your engine was vandalized - $400 damage:

- If you had no insurance (insurance choice A) - deduct $400 from what is left of your money.

- If you had $200 deductible (insurance choice B) - deduct $200 from what is left of your money.

- If you had non-deductible (insurance choice C) - your insurance pays for repairs.

If you wrote III, they skipped your vehicle.

If you wrote IV, your car was stolen, and it was not recovered:

- If you had no insurance - deduct $1000 from what is left of your money.

- If you had $200 deductible - deduct $200 from what is left of your money.

- If you had non-deductible - your insurance pays for new vehicle.

Write the number 4 on your piece of paper and then write how much money you have left after taking care of this.

- If you had no damage - Everything is ok. Your car is still ready to go.

- If your tires were slit - It will take the tire store 1 day to fix your car.

- If your engine was vandalized - The auto repair shop will take 1 week to fix your car.

- If your car was stolen - The car dealer will take 1 month to get you a different car.

Here are some problems some people might experience after a crime:

1. Victims might emotionally struggle to figure out why it happened to them.

2. Victims may find it difficult to trust anyone again.

3. Victims may have to buy more insurance.

4. Victims may have to depend upon others for rides and feel like they are a burden on their friends.

5. Victims might isolate themselves and stay inside all the time.

6. Victims might be late for school or work or lose work time and wages.

7. Victims may have to pay medical costs.

8. Victims may have trouble sleeping.

9. Victims may blame themselves and be embarrassed.

10. Victims may have to pay for losses out of their own pocket.

11. Victims may be very angry or sad or worried or afraid.

12. Victims may pay insurance deductibles or have their insurance rates go up.

13. Victims and all other taxpayers may have their taxes go up because of the need for more law enforcement and prisons.

14. Victims may lose personal items that cannot be replaced.

15. Victims may have to walk.

16. Victims may feel powerless.

17. Victims might have to move.

18. Victims may have to clean up after vandalism.

These are things that happen in neighborhoods because of crime. Write the number 5 on your paper and then the number from the list above that you might have just experienced after the vandalism in this game. Next to each write a little about why you think that you might experience such things.

Even if you had no damage done during an incident of vandalism in your neighborhood, how might it affect you anyway? Write the number 6 on your paper and explain your thoughts on this.

It is time again for insurance payments. You can change your policy if you want. However, if you filed a claim against the insurance company last time, you will have your insurance raised $100 this time. In other words, if the insurance company had to pay anything out on you, your rates go up. Your options are:

A. No insurance (no costs)

B. $200 deductible insurance, costs$100 or $200 - if previously filed a claim.

C. non-deductible insurance, costs $300 or $400 - if previously filed a claim.

Write the number 7 on your paper. Then pick your insurance policy and with its letter (A, B, or C) on your paper. Then subtract the cost of that policy from how much money you have left and write the answer on your paper. If you do not have any money, you will have to skip insurance.

Here is your policy.

While you were all away at a church picnic, the same people were partying again. They swept through the church parking lot, vandalizing, and stealing vehicles. When you returned on the church bus you saw what had happened.

Write the number 8 on your piece of paper and then randomly pick the Roman Numeral I or II or III or IV and write it down.

If you wrote I, they skipped your vehicle.

If you wrote II, your car was stolen, and it was not recovered:

- If you had no insurance - deduct $1000 from what is left of your money.

- If you had $200 deductible - deduct $200 from what is left of your money.

- If you had non-deductible - your insurance pays for new vehicle.

If you wrote III, your tires were slit - $200 damage:

- If you had no insurance - deduct $200 from what is left of your money.

- If you had $200 deductible - deduct $200 from what is left of your money.

- If you had non-deductible - your insurance pays for repairs.

If you wrote the letter IV, your engine was vandalized - $400 damage:

- If you had no insurance - deduct $400 from what is left of your money.

- If you had $200 deductible - deduct $200 from what is left of your money.

- If you had non-deductible - your insurance pays for repairs.

Write the number 9 on your piece of paper and then write how much money you have left after taking care of this. If you have to borrow money, write how much you had to borrow (along with the word "BORROWED").

Subtract the money you have left from $1000 (your original amount of money). If you had to borrow money, subtract that amount as well. This is how much money you lost to vandalism. Next, divide your answer by 8.

Write the number 10 on your paper and then write your answer. Also, write what you might do with the money you lost to vandalism if you had never lost it.

If you made $8.00 per hour, this is how many hours you would have worked during the last year to pay for the fun the vandals were having.

Write the number 11 on your paper and then write how much money do you think most people would pay for theft and vandalism insurance if no one ever stole or

vandalized cars?

Write the number 12 on your paper. Might there be some people who are afraid to go out after dark because of crime? Who might they be? Are their fears justified? Are they still afraid whether their fears are justified or not? Write your answers and explain them.

Write the number 13 on your paper and then write what you think victims feel about people who harm them or their property. Why do they feel that way? Write your answers and explain them.

Write the number 14 on your paper and then write how a crime can tum violent even when the person committing it does not intend beforehand for that to happen?

It is time again for insurance payments. You can change your policy if you want. The good news is that your rate will not go up if you previously filed a claim against the insurance company. The bad news is, since your area is so full of crime, the insurance company has decided to raise the base rates by $100 for everyone. Your options are:

    A. Not buy insurance (no cost)

    B. Buy $200 deductible for $200

    C. Buy non-deductible for $400

Write the number 15 on your paper. Then pick your insurance policy and write its letter on your paper. Then subtract the cost of that policy from how much money you have left and write the answer on your paper. If you do not have any money, you will have to skip insurance.

Here is your policy

Write the number 16 on your piece of paper and then randomly pick the Roman Numeral I or II or III or IV and write it down.

While you were all at a Crime Watch meeting, the same criminals swept through your area, vandalizing, and stealing vehicles. When you left the meeting, you saw the damage.

.

If you wrote I, your engine was vandalized - $400 damage:

    - If you had no insurance - deduct $400 from what is left of your money.

    - If you had $200 deductible - deduct $200 from what is left of your money.

    - If you had non-deductible - your insurance pays for repairs.

If you wrote II, your tires were slit - $200 damage:

    - If you had no insurance - deduct $200 from what is left of your money.

    - If you had $200 deductible - deduct $200 from what is left of your money.

    - If you had non-deductible - your insurance pays for repairs.

If you wrote III, they skipped your vehicle. However, your grandmother's only picture of her husband (your grandfather, who was killed in the war) was stolen.

If you wrote IV, your tires were slit - $200 damage:

- If you had no insurance - deduct $200 from what is left of your money.

- If you had $200 deductible - deduct $200 from what is left of your money.

- If you had non-deductible - your insurance pays for repairs.

Write the number 17 on your piece of paper and then write how much money you have left after taking care of this. If you have to borrow money, write how much you had to borrow (along with the word "BORROWED").

How would you feel, after all of this you got a phone call and found out that you were fired for missing too much work? Or, evicted for missing rent payments? Or, have people thinking you did something wrong to have all this happen to you? This is what they mean by revictimization. Write the number 18 on your paper and then write how you would feel.

How did you do? Sometimes, even the people who handle their money the best cannot do well when it comes to being a victim.

One of the vandals got caught.

"I'm sorry for what I did. I was drunk. I know that it was wrong, but at least I only messed with their cars. It didn't cause them that much trouble."

Write the number 19 on your paper and then write what you would tell the judge about your experience. What all happened to you? How do you feel? What do you think the judge should do to the vandal?

Write the number 20 on your paper and then write what the victim of your current offense would tell the judge about their experience. What all happened to them? How do they feel? What do you believe they think the judge should have done to you?

Remember, even if you had no specific victim, we have seen how crime can affect everyone in the community. If your crime did not have a specific victim, write instead how what you did caused your community to be a worse place to live.

11 Being Part Of A System

If you line up a bunch of dominos and push the one on the end over, they each fall in turn, one after the other.

Write the number 1 on a piece of paper and then write what some people call this effect.

Some people call it the domino effect. These dominos are like a system. Even though they are separate pieces, they work together as a team. Their final outcome is that all the dominos fall over.

There are many systems, people that work together for some final outcome. For example:

A. The school system (principal, teachers, janitors, cooks, clerks, etc.).

B. The court system (judges, defense attorneys, prosecutors, bailiffs, clerks, etc.).

C. The social security system (administrators, clerks, accountants, etc.).

D. The probation system (probation officers, secretaries, supervisors, etc.).

Write the number 2 on your piece of paper and then list 10 people that are needed to keep a city bus system going.

Here are some answers that other people often mention:

     bus drivers

     mechanics

     secretaries

     administrators

     accountants

     purchasing agents

     foremen

     janitors

Did you include riders?

Now, what would happen to the domino effect if one or two dominos were removed from the middle? Write the number 3 on your piece of paper and then write your answer.

Did you write something to the effect that the dominos would stop in the middle and the system would come to a halt.

Each person in a system does something to keep the system going. If that part of the system is removed, the system eventually breaks down.

Would the bus system eventually come to a halt if there were no bus drivers, mechanics, secretaries, administrators, accountants, purchasing agents, foremen, or janitors? How about riders? Would the system eventually come to a halt if there were no riders? Write the number 4 on your paper and then your thoughts on these questions.

Now we are going to switch gears a little. Imagine you know someone who sells guns illegally. He sold a gun to a guy who then robbed a restaurant. The guy who sold the gun did not know what the customer was going to use it for, but he knew that it was against the law to sell it to him this way and that his customers don't want the law to know they have a gun.

Write the number 5 on your paper and then answer these questions:

A. Is the guy who sold the gun part of a system? Explain why you think this.

B. How might the guy who sold the gun feel about what happened to the victims of the robbery?

C. How might the people who were robbed at gunpoint feel about the robber?

D. How might the people who were robbed at gunpoint feel about the guy who sold the illegal gun? Do you think that their feelings are justified? The seller didn't actually commit the robbery.

E. Looking at it from a systems perspective, how do other customers of illegal guns contribute to the robbery?

Next, the guy sold a gun to a man who went into a schoolyard and randomly killed three children.

Write the number 6 on your paper and then answer these questions:

A. How might the guy who sold the gun feel about what happened to the victims and their families?

B. How might the parents of the dead children feel about the killer?

C. How might the parents of the dead children feel about the guy who sold the illegal gun? Do you think that their feelings are justified?

D. How might the guy who sold the illegal gun feel if one of the children killed was his little sister?

E. Looking at it from a systems perspective, how do other customers of illegal guns contribute to the shootings?

In the first scene of the movie *Losing Isaiah*, a mother is nursing her little baby. They are in a rundown apartment in a rundown part of town. The mother feels bad because she is addicted to cocaine and hasn't used it for a while. Her baby is fussy because he was born addicted. She leaves to get a fix and must take her baby with her.

The mother needs to leave her baby some place while she goes to get her crack. She finds a cardboard box in a pile of trash. She gently puts Isaiah in the box and pulls his blanket over him. Isaiah is crying and she tries to comfort him as best she can. However, the cravings are strong, and she wants to find some crack. She covers the box with a piece of cardboard and rushes off to get high.

The next day, Isaiah is still in the box. His mother passed out after getting high. Two garbage collectors, going about their everyday business, put the box that still had Isaiah in it in the rear of the garbage truck. One of the men pulls the lever to compact the trash, when the cover of the box falls off and Isaiah begins to cry. The garbage man looks in horror as he sees the giant metal compactor about to smash the baby. "Stop the truck. Stop the truck."

Write the number 7 on your paper and then answer these questions:

A. How do you think the mother felt about leaving her baby in the trash?

B. Do you think she planned to have harm come to her son? What do you believe she was thinking?

C. Was her son harmed in any way regardless of what she intended?

D. Is the harm done to victims less injurious because the people who harm them did not intend to do so?

Back to the movie *Losing Isaiah.* The garbage men stop the truck just in time and get Isaiah out. An ambulance rushes him to a hospital. A doctor rushes over and starts to attend to him. He shouts out orders for blood and oxygen.

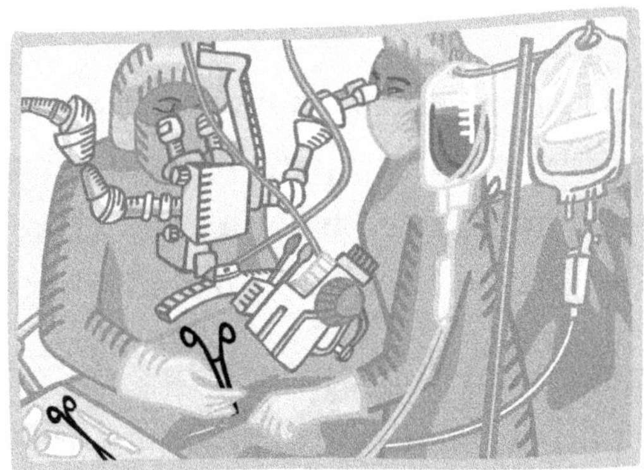

A social worker comes over. The doctor says that the baby is not breathing on his own and that she should "sign off on him." That means that the doctor doesn't believe the baby will live and that he should be taken off of life support and allowed to die. The social worker replies, "Why don't we just dump him back in the dumpster?" To which the doctor replies, "All right, go ahead and play god."

Write the number 8 on your paper and then answer these questions:

A. The doctor asked the social worker to "sign off" on Isaiah. He was asking her to just let the baby die. What do you think about the doctor?

B. Why do you think he was so callous, so heartless?

C. Do you think he was always so cold hearted?

D. What might he have told himself that made it less hurtful to him that the baby should be allowed to die?

E. How do you think finding a baby in the trash affected the garbage men?

F. How do you think a newspaper story about a baby in the trash affected the readers?

G. Do you think these kinds of incidents lead to stricter laws or laws creating more treatment centers?

Write the number 9 on your paper and then answer these questions:

A. Who paid for the ambulance ride?

B. Who paid the doctor bills?

C. Who paid the hospital bills?

Think about this the next time you look at the tax deductions on your paycheck.

Write the number 10 on your piece of paper and answer whether you think illegal drugs have a system to support them. Explain your answer.

1. Growers

2.

3.

4.

5.

6.

7. Users

Write the number 11 on your paper and then make a list of all of the people necessary to keep the illegal drug system going.

Write the number 12 on your paper and then answer these questions:

A. Looking at it from a systems perspective, how does the person who sold illegal drugs to Isaiah's mother contribute to Isaiah being put in the trash?

B. Looking at it from a systems perspective, how do other drug users contribute to Isaiah being put in the trash?

C. How is a person who is part of a drug system, but denies contributing to the negative outcomes (like Isaiah being put in the trash), similar to the illegal gun dealer?

What is the disadvantage of becoming a person who contributes to the harming of others and not feel bad about it. Write the number 13 on your paper and then write your thoughts about this.

12 Finding Your Way

Imagine a friend called you on the phone and asked for directions. She wanted you to make her a map. What three things would you need to know in order to make her the map? Write the number 1 on a piece of paper and then write your answer.

Did you answer:

    1) Where is she?

    2) Where is she going?

    3) How to get from where she is to where she is going?

Now, on another piece of paper, make a map from your home to one of your favorite places. Put your home at the bottom of the paper and your favorite place at the top. Make lines for the streets you will use. Make sure you label the streets.

Look at your map. Find the first major intersection. If you went the wrong way at that intersection, what would be something that you would see that made you say, "Hey- I'm going the wrong way"? Write the number 2 on your paper and write that down.

Now imagine a Martian coming to Earth. He didn't know anything about Earthlings and what they do. You had to explain everything to him. Here are some things you might have to explain.

If you walked into a home in which the husband and wife didn't get along: What would you see and hear that let you know that that was the case? How do people feel when they are not getting along? What might be some of their thoughts? Write the number 3 on your paper and then write your answers. Be specific.

If you walked into a home in which the residents were unemployed: What would you see and hear that let you know that that was the case? How do people feel when they are not working? What might be some of their thoughts? Write the number 4 on your paper and then write your answers. Be specific.

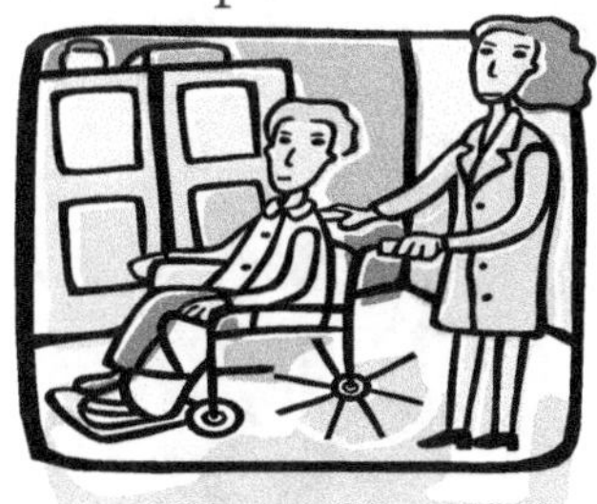

If you walked into a home in which one of the residents was sick: What would you see and hear that let you know that that was the case? How do people feel when they are sick? What might be some of their thoughts? Write the number 5 on your paper and then write your answers. Be specific.

If you walked into a home in which one of the residents had low self-esteem: What would you see and hear that let you know that that was the case? How do people feel when they have low self-esteem? What might be some of their thoughts? Write the number 6 on your paper and then write your answers. Be specific.

If you walked into a home in which residents used alcohol or other drugs and they did not consider it a problem: What would you see and hear that let you know that that was the case? How do people feel when they drink or use other drugs, and they do not consider it a problem? What might be some of their thoughts? Write the number 7 on your paper and then write your answers. Be specific.

If you walked into a home in which residents used alcohol or other drugs and they did consider it a problem: What would you see and hear that let you know that that was the case? How do people feel when they drink or use other drugs, and they consider it a problem? What might be some of their thoughts? Write the number 8 on your paper and then write your answers. Be specific.

Write the number 9 on your paper and then write your thoughts on how these are all related. For example, heavy drinking can cause work problems, which can cause marital problems and so on.

Now you walked into a home in which the husband and wife get along: What would you see and hear that let you know that that was the case? How do people feel when they are getting along? What might be some of their thoughts? Write the number 10 on your paper and then write your answers. Be specific.

If you walked into a home in which the residents were employed: What would you see and hear that let you know that that was the case? How do people feel when they are working? What might be some of their thoughts? Write the number 11 on your paper and then write your answers. Be specific.

If you walked into a home in which the residents were healthy: What would you see and hear that let you know that that was the case? How do people feel when they are healthy? What might be some of their thoughts? Write the number 12 on your paper and then write your answers. Be specific.

If you walked into a home in which one of the residents had good self-esteem: What would you see and hear that let you know that that was the case? How do people feel when they have good self-esteem? What might be some of their thoughts? Write the number 13 on your paper and then write your answers. Be specific.

If you walked into a home in which residents who once had an alcohol or other drug problem and now are sober or straight: What would you see and hear that let you know that that was the case? How do people feel when they are in recovery? What might be some of their thoughts? Write the number 14 on your paper and then write your answers. Be specific.

You know what your main problem area is like when it is bad. You know what you want life to be like when your problem is fixed. Take the map you drew earlier and put how that problem looks now on the bottom of the page. That is where you are.

You can draw a picture or use words. Put how that problem will look when it is fixed on the top of the paper. That is where you are going. Again, you can draw a picture or use words.

Then cross out the street names on your map and rename them with the names of things you have to do in order to fix your problem (get from where you are to where you want to be). For example, Get a Job Street or Go to Drug Treatment Street.)

Look at your map. Find the first major intersection. If you went the wrong way at that intersection, what would you be doing? For example, the wrong turn might be hanging around with old friends. Write the number 15 on your paper and write that down.

Then with your wrong turn, think about what you might see and hear that would make you think that going down this street was okay rather than heading toward your goal. How do you feel when you are heading down the wrong street? What might be some of your thoughts? Write the number 16 on your paper and then write your answers.

Now do that for each tempting wrong turn on your map.

You now have a map that will help you get what you really want out of life.

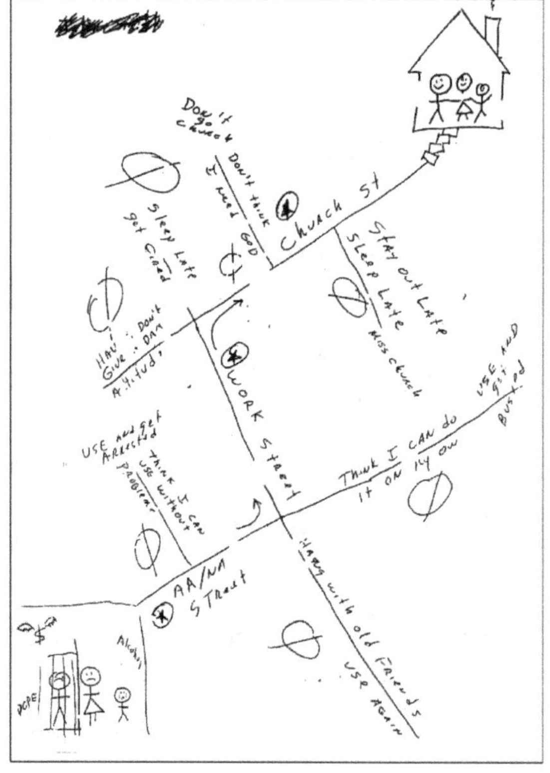